THE RESPONSE TO MEPROBAMATE—
A PREDICTIVE ANALYSIS

THE RESPONSE
TO MEPROBAMATE—
A PREDICTIVE
ANALYSIS

J. R. WITTENBORN, Ph.D.

University Professor of Psychology and Education
Director, Rutgers Interdisciplinary Research Center
Rutgers—The State University
New Brunswick, New Jersey

RAVEN PRESS · NEW YORK

Standard Book Number 911216–11–1
Library of Congress catalog card number 70–107228

Preface

The present account describes an attempt to conceptualize the effect of a psychotropic drug in terms which could eventually be applied to the anticipation of the response of the individual patient. This predictive interest has its origin in the fact that all patients with a given set of symptoms do not respond equally well to a generally efficacious pharmacotherapy. It is believed that predictive insights which could be used to anticipate the response of the individual patient would not only contribute to the optimal use of the drug in clinical situations, but might also lead to advances in our understanding of the essential nature of drug effects and of the behavioral disorders which they ameliorate.

Although the present effort is obviously predictive in its implications, it differs from most current predictive studies in the particular respect that it does not attempt to establish a quantified statement of a pragmatic relationship between predictive variables and criteria of therapeutic efficacy. Instead, it strives to establish a concept which succinctly summarizes the general quality of the therapeutic effect and which leads to an anticipation of the conditions under which the effect is most probable.

In order to pursue this integrative purpose, the published accounts of controlled studies of meprobamate were subjected to systematic scrutiny. As a first step in this scrutiny, the animal studies and the experimental studies of normal human subjects were examined for consistencies which, in the light of clinical material already familiar to the writer, could generate integrating concepts. From such materials it was possible to formulate a suitably comprehensive concept, and its consequences were deduced for many common clinical situations. These deductions were expressed as hypotheses. The vast remaining literature of controlled clinical studies was then examined from the standpoint of whether the

6

reported experimental results appeared to be consistent or inconsistent with pertinent hypotheses.

Thus it is apparent that this approach to predictive insights requires a substantial and varied experimental literature. There are several drugs for which such a literature is available, but perhaps the most substantial literature has been developed for meprobamate, one of the older psychotropics, a minor tranquilizer still in general use. It is hoped that the present report may lead other investigators to test some of these hypotheses and may stimulate comparable efforts to conceptualize the effects of other established psychotropic drugs. In this way, additional specific clinically-pertinent hypotheses may become available for test.

The present account is brief, but it is the result of persistent effort on the part of several persons. The writer is particularly indebted to Mr. Joseph Potterfield, who contributed substantially in the preliminary search of the literature for controlled studies that met the writer's criteria with respect to size of sample and adequacy of controls. In addition, the resources of the library of Wallace Laboratories are gratefully acknowledged. Not to be forgotten are the loyal efforts of the writer's secretary, Gloria Light, and whatever clarity the manuscript possesses is in substantial measure the result of the patient editing of Sarah A. Wittenborn.

Responsibility for the conceptualizations and interpretations offered here must be borne by the writer alone, however, and it is his hope that the investigators cited will be comfortable with the manner in which their contributions have been applied to the present system of hypotheses.

J. R. Wittenborn

New Brunswick, New Jersey
March 27, 1969

Contents

Chapter I

INTRODUCTION

The present survey is a part of a program of inquiry concerned with the selection of the optimal pharmacotherapy for the individual. Some of the individual differences in therapeutic response can be explained in terms of the nature of the presenting symptoms, but even among patients whose patterns of symptomatic manifestation appear to be uniform there are important differences in the manner in which they respond to a given psychotropic agent. For certain drugs, predictive correlates of some of these differences have been identified, and they suggest that whether a given pharmacotherapy will have its expected consequences may depend somewhat on the history of the illness and the functional significance of the symptomatic aberrations in the individual's system of defenses. Conceivably a given symptom may have different adaptive significance in different persons. Perhaps the fact that a given psychotropic may be effective in controlling the symptom for one patient and not for another could be explained in terms of the possibility that the symptom serves different adaptive requirements in the two individuals. Such a possibility implies that it is not the symptom *per se* but a symptom-producing, adaptive requirement that is modified by a given psychotropic agent, i.e., a metabolic complex or a motivational disposition that may be modified by the psychotropic agent in question.

The pursuit of predictive insights which may be used to anticipate the individual's response to a given psychotropic may follow either of two courses. One course requires the development of new data; the other course rests upon a review of the reports of prior investigations.

When the body of published material is scant, there is no alternative to an empirical, data-generating, research approach. In such an approach, one uses clues, however fragmentary and dubious, to formulate two sets of variables. One set of variables, known as criteria, should sample the kinds of pertinent changes which may be expected in consequence of the pharmacotherapy. The other set of variables, hopefully called predictors, should represent the kinds of conditions, circumstances, and background factors which may be expected to qualify, by either enhancing or suppressing, the individual's response to the pharmacotherapy. Guided by these two lists (criteria and predictors), an investigator can undertake a standardized treatment and assessment procedure which, in time, will generate enough data to show possible associations between some of the predictors and some of the criteria of effect. In this formal way, the investigator develops a body of information which he, in his data analyses, can survey for the purpose of identifying any relationships between predictors and criteria. Such relationships become the subject for replicative study, and if the relationships are confirmed, they can be used with varying degrees of confidence as a guide for anticipating an individual's response to clinical use of the psychotropic substance.

Sound empirical investigations are invariably time consuming, and years may pass before an investigator can generate enough information to establish verifiable, well conceptualized, clinically applicable predictive relationships. For this reason, all procedures that could shorten and perhaps sharpen the search for concepts to be used in clinical prediction must be explored. The use of some of the older pharmacotherapies is now well into the second decade, and the published reports of controlled studies are sufficiently numerous to offer a potential source of empirical relationships that could be applied to the predictive purpose.

It is proposed, therefore, that the published literature be surveyed for the purpose of sorting the various empirical relationships in the hope that sufficient consistency may be found to provide a basis for predictive formulations. It is possible that such a review of controlled studies could lead to insights that would serve to unify the diverse, unrelated mass of information from various reports and to rationalize the conditions under which the most probable response to the specific drug occurs. Specifically, the identification of the general conditions under which a response to a specific drug will occur and the conditions under which a response is improbable could provide empirical basis for the predictive anticipation of the individual's response to the drug.

Although a search of the established literature for consistencies that might lead to insights has the appeal of economy, it is fraught with hazards and uncertainties. The research literature is made up of fallible reports; it is heterogeneous in nature and was not generated from the standpoint of the requirement of the investigator who will search the reports for consistent or unifying trends. The interpretive use of the research literature must be guided, therefore, by an explicit awareness of the biases and limitations of the literature as a body of knowledge. Certainly it cannot be expected to represent the universe of pertinent information. Perhaps the greatest limitation lies in the *criteria* for therapeutic effect. The selection of criteria rests on both explicit and implicit presuppositions. These presuppositions come from many sources. Some are based on the speculations of the biochemists and the pharmacologists who developed the drug; others appear to be based upon the strategy of the marketing departments of the pharmaceutical house that owns the drug. Specifically, often the direction taken in exploratory research reflects a two-fold desire to define a product that can be integrated with other products presently provided by the drug house and to preempt a potential market or to share an established market in which other drug houses participate. Investigators themselves use the procedures with which they are familiar and are not always sensitive to consideration of reliability or pertinence of the question at issue. The information found in the research report may be influenced more by the drug market and by the convenience of the investigators than by the implications of the clues provided in the emerging research reports. Thus the criteria tend to be inappropriately selected and, in addition, are usually psychometrically fallible. Because of the arbitrary if not inappropriate selections of criteria, it seems probable that every psychotropic drug has a potential for more certain and powerful effects than will be revealed in the literature.

The published literature contains relatively little negative material, and the conditions and the criteria that do not show a response to a drug may not be reported. To some extent, this is unfortunate because often the nature of a drug effect is best defined in terms of contrast between actual changes that result from the drug and conceivable changes that do not result from the drug.

Some of the customs of reporting drug effects obscure more than they reveal. For example, the practice of reporting drug effects in terms of group averages seems to carry with it the implication that every member of the group changes by the average amount. Often, however, many, if not most, of the group are not involved in the change, and the magnitude of the change among the responsive persons in the sample is greatly understated by the average. The use of averages with the implication that all members of the sample are essentially the same in their response does not lead to a scrutiny of the characteristics of the particularly sensitive or insensitive members of the sample.

Although most investigators do not describe distinctions between the good and poor responders in their sample, the various investigations do differ from each other in the composition of their sample. Contrasts between effects reported for different samples can provide some indication either of the kinds of samples that are most responsive and can yield some clues to the patient characteristics, or of the conditions that will be found in the persons most likely to respond.

Because of the limitations of the criteria of effect and the tendency to describe effect in terms of group averages, the available literature does not provide a proper basis for developing a meaningful assessment of the efficacy of a psychotropic drug. If efficacy could be gauged in terms of the most sensitive criteria and with respect to the most responsive subjects, it seems likely that the literature would be found to have underestimated the efficacy of most, if not all, of the psychopharmacotherapeutic agents.

Upon reflection, however, it is apparent that the question of therapeutic efficacy is a riddle of paradoxes. The question "What is the effect of a drug?" is an incomplete and inappropriate, if not meaningless, question. The effect that will be observed depends upon the nature of the sample, the conditions of administration, choice of criteria, the dosage regimen, and the time orientation which guided the assessment. Is it speed of effect, duration of effect, maximal ultimate power of effect? How is ultimate power of effect defined? Is it in terms of the number of persons involved, in terms of the variety of behaviors modified, or in terms of the resistance of the symptoms controlled? In general, when one asks about effect, one implies an interest in what effects, for whom, and under what conditions. It appears, therefore, that the question of the effect of the drug is not a question which is directly answered, but a question for which the answer accrues through time, and the nature of the answer, as well as the meaning of the question, matures and modifies with cumulative experience.

Thus the drug image which is provided by the early research determines the therapeutic use which will be sanctioned by the Food and Drug Administration (FDA) and the manner in which it is perceived by the consumer in consequence of the marketing efforts of the manufacturer. In time, however, it may be apparent to some investigators, at least, that the FDA was not supplied with material most appropriate for recognizing the drug's greatest therapeutic promise and that the drug has been committed to a role from which constructive retrieval may be virtually impossible. Accordingly, a retrospective scrutiny of the accumulated published literature must necessarily come too late to serve a maximal value. It can be hoped, however, that refinements in our concepts of the action of a drug can always accrue to the benefit of the patient and the peace of mind of the clinician.

Beyond the therapeutic advantage of predictive knowledge concerning for whom and under what conditions a therapeutic effect may be expected, the conceptualizations that may be stimulated by a knowledge of predictive relationships contribute to the strength of the emerging discipline of clinical psychopharmacology and may be justifiable as an academic pursuit *per se*.

Several conditions led to the choice of meprobamate as the drug for the present predictive survey. A most important consideration was the size of the literature. Meprobamate is a well established drug which has been applied to a diversity of situations, and a large and diversified body of published research reports is available. Since many of these reports have appeared within the last decade, a very substantial number of them comprises controlled studies based on adequate samples and reported in a manner which includes usefully detailed description of the sample and of the procedures. Meprobamate seems particularly suitable from the standpoint of a predictive inquiry because it is not a powerful drug with an invariable effect. Instead, it is known to be a minor tranquilizer which is effective in some situations but not in others and is commonly observed to be more effective for some persons than for others. Although the possible applications of meprobamate provide contrasts in therapeutic consequence, there seems to be no accepted general concept which can be used to anticipate those particular situations in which or those particular individuals for whom it would be most effective.

The plan for the present scrutiny of trends and predictive formulations involved the following considerations:

1. Only controlled studies of behavioral criteria were examined.
2. Although no interpretable reports of adequate studies were disregarded and an effort was made to represent the literature comprehensively, the survey sought predictive patterns and need not be and makes no claim for being exhaustive.
3. The general approach comprised three phases:
   a. The first phase comprised the search for consistencies in the published literature. A scrutiny of animal studies proceeded to the studies of normal human subjects and then to a reflective consideration of the familiar clinical findings.
   b. The second phase represented an attempt to conceptualize whatever consistencies emerged in the course of the first phase, to express the concepts in terms of formal generalizations and then to deduce their consequences for all familiar clinical situations.
   c. The third phase comprised a review of all available reports of controlled clinical studies with the explicit purpose of determining which, if any, of the predictive deductions or hypotheses were consistent with the results of each of the investigations.

Thus, the nonclinical literature and the familiar clinical effects were reviewed to reveal consistencies on which generalizing inferences were based. The specific consequences deduced from these inferences were then examined in the light of a rather comprehensive survey of the clinical literature. In this way, the inferences provided the conceptualizations, and the consequent deductions provided the hypotheses for guiding a comprehensive review of the clinical literature.

Chapter II

ANIMAL STUDIES

Fighting Behavior

The various reports of controlled investigations describing the effect of meprobamate on fighting and related behavior are not altogether consistent in their implications. As a result, the question of the effect of meprobamate on aggression is surrounded with ambiguities and qualifications.

Janssen et al. (1960) described a study wherein fighting was induced by isolation. In this kind of fighting behavior, meprobamate did not appear to have a selective effect, and fighting behavior was suppressed at doses which begin to have a neurological effect.

In the same year, Mantegazzini et al. (1960) reported that meprobamate had the effect of reducing fighting behavior in mice that had been kept in isolation five days prior to exposure to an opponent. They found that injected dosages of approximately 78 mg. per kilograms were sufficient to abolish aggressiveness in half of the animals tested. Among these animals, there was no indication of incoordination, and it was reported that the aggressiveness returned three or four hours after treatment.

In 1960, Cook and Weidley described the effect of meprobamate on pairs of mice that had been maintained in isolation. They reported that two hundred mg. per kilograms of meprobamate orally administered are required in order to suppress fighting response in fifty per cent of the mice.

In 1966, DaVanzo et al. studied the fighting behavior of isolated mice, and among the variables they examined were the effects of various pharmacological agents including meprobamate. It was reported that

15

meprobamate suppressed fighting behavior at about the same dosage level as the neurotoxic dose. Here again it is implied or at least may be inferred that meprobamate may not be a specific inhibitor of aggressive behavior, but may retard aggressive behavior perhaps in the same manner that other behavior is retarded at dosages at the sedative level and certainly at the neurotoxic level.

The reduction of fighting time in mice that had been isolated was used in a comparative study by Scriabine and Blake (1962). The drug was administered intraperitoneally, and it was found that meprobamate would reduce fighting time at dosages as low as 50 mg. per kilogram, but when the dosage was raised to as much as 200 mg. per kilogram there was impairment of motor activity. The authors believe that reduction of fighting time is a more sensitive measure of tranquilizing effect than is reduction of fighting incidence.

The literature of the effect of meprobamate on fighting behavior refers to several different conditions and qualities including the provocative circumstances. In 1959, Tedeschi et al. described the use of meprobamate in the antagonism of fighting behavior induced by delivering two minutes of continuous foot shock to mice and then recording the number of fighting episodes.

In 1966, Brittain compared meprobamate with mephenesin and an experimental compound. In this report the amount of drug required to suppress fighting induced by foot shock was expressed as a ratio of the amount of drug required to induce paralysis. Meprobamate at oral dose of 62 mg. per kilogram of body weight was found to suppress fighting without producing paralysis, but for the other two drugs the suppression of fighting occurred at a dosage level approaching that required to produce paralysis. Meprobamate was described as having a relatively selective action approximately three times more effective than the other two compounds.

Chen et al. (1963) also described meprobamate as having a suppressive effect on fighting behavior. In this study mice were preconditioned by exposing them to a three-minute period of foot shock before the test. Aggression was considered to be suppressed when there were fewer than three fighting episodes during a three-minute test period. Several different dosage levels were employed, and the data were used to estimate the dosage level at which fighting would be suppressed in fifty per cent of the pairs. This was found to be about 122 mg. per kilogram in this sample of mice. The authors discussed the suppressive effect of meprobamate in terms of sedation as contrasted with hypnosis, but apparently they did not construe their results to be specifically pertinent to fighting behavior. Instead they regarded the suppression of fighting behavior as some sort of indication of general sedation.

Heise and Boff (1961) studied the taming effect of several pharmacologic agents on vicious mature monkeys. They reported substantial taming effect for chlordiazepoxide and phenobarbital but no visible taming effect for chlorpromazine and meprobamate.

Fear and Avoidance

The literature contains several accounts of the effect of meprobamate on the emotional responses of animals, particularly fear-like responses. In 1963, Plotnikoff reported separate experiments in which he assessed different aspects of fear-like responses. One was a study of generalized fright response where various forms of behavior were graded to form a total score; another had to do with observing the presence or absence of convulsions. In each of these studies the dose was varied systematically in order to examine the suppressive effect of meprobamate as a function of dosage. The generalized fright response was antagonized by chlorpromazine, reserpine, and by meprobamate also. In all cases the righting reflex was retained indicating that the suppression of fear could not be accounted for in terms of hypnotic effects. In this study, groups of ten mice were used and they served as their own controls. In the anticonvulsant study, the three compounds were again employed and were found to be effective in suppressing this aspect of the audiogenic response. Two strains of mice were employed, and it was observed that the two strains were not equally susceptible to the medications. Chlorpromazine was found to be an effective suppressor in one strain only; meprobamate was found to be more effective in one strain than the other, while reserpine was found to be equally effective in the two strains.

In 1960, Hess reported a study of the effect of meprobamate on imprinting in ducklings. This study was undertaken on the theory that imprinting and the associated social responses that occur in very young animals is possible because it occurs before the intrinsic fearful and avoidant responses make their appearance. On this basis, it was anticipated that if meprobamate were effective in reducing fear in young ducklings, imprinting could occur at a later age than would otherwise be possible. It was concluded that meprobamate inhibited emotionality and interfered with imprinting as well. It is not clear, however, on what basis emotionality was evaluated.

The effect of meprobamate on paroxysmal inhibition has been reported by Davis (1963). This kind of inhibition or freezing usually occurs in the presence of threatening environmental stimuli. The response is hypothesized as being accompanied by or perhaps triggered by hippocampal hyperactivity and subsequent decreasing activity of the reticular activating system. Regardless of the effect of meprobamate on these nervous structures *per se,* it was found that meprobamate did decrease the period of immobility induced by holding the animal in a supine position.

Jacob and Michaud (1960) considered exhaustion time in swimming as a measure of emotionality. They found in control mice that the average exhaustion time was about five and one-half minutes, while in meprobamate-treated mice the exhaustion time was seven or more minutes. It was noted that the favorable effect in the meprobamate group was accompanied by a reduction in the initial agitation which characterized the control group. Morphine also was observed to have a beneficial effect on exhaustion time, but not as great as that of meprobamate.

In a later study, Jacob and Michaud (1961) confirmed the beneficial effect of meprobamate on the exhaustion time of swimming mice. Again they noted the partial suppression of the initial agitation and ascribed some of the beneficial effect to this action. Thus, it is apparent that meprobamate reduced some of the initial avoidant agitation that occurred when mice were placed in water.

Most of the controlled studies of animal response to meprobamate appear to have involved the reduction of avoidant responses. In 1960, Hughes and Kopmann described a study where young rats were placed in a compartment with a grilled floor, and after exposure to five seconds of a warning light, shock was delivered to the grill. Concurrent with the warning light, a door was opened to two chambers, one which had an insulated floor and the other which had a charged grid as a floor. The dependent variable was the number of trials in which the rat stayed in the original box and took the shock without leaving the box. The disposition of the animal to remain in the box and take the shock instead of leaving to avoid the shock appeared to be an increasing function of dosage level with barely noticeable effects at 50 mg. dosage and prompt and conspicuous effects at 100 mg. One interesting feature was the observation that after four hours the animals returned to their normal level of response and left the original charged chamber.

In the same year, however, Lynch et al. (1960) reported negative results after using a rod test to examine the effect of meprobamate on a conditioned avoidant response. Meprobamate was not found to be significantly better than placebo in increasing the latency of the animals jumping from the charged grid to the pole.

In 1960, Niki reported two experiments which are pertinent to the possible reduction of acquired avoidant responses as a consequence of meprobamate. In the first experiment, a simple escape apparatus was employed, and it was found that animals receiving meprobamate were not reliably different from the control animals either with respect to the latency of their escape response or the readiness with which the extinction recovered. It should be noted that this was a simple escape situation and did not involve any avoidance learning. In Niki's second experiment, a discrimination apparatus was employed in an avoidance learning procedure. It was found that the meprobamate group made significantly more errors than the control group and required significantly more trials to reach a criterion of nine consecutive errorless trials. This report suggested that although meprobamate may not interfere with the animals' escape from pain, it does interfere with the acquisition of acquired avoidance responses.

In 1960, Olds and Travis described the effect of meprobamate on self-stimulation behavior of rats in which electrodes had been implanted in the hypothalamus. Among implanted animals that are trained to deliver stimulation to themselves by pressing a bar, stimulation of certain specific locations in this area of the brain leads to rapid self-stimulation. In nearby locations, however, stimulation delivered by the implanted electrode produces strong escape reactions as if the animals were in intense pain. Meprobamate was found to facilitate the self-stimulating responses among those animals where the electrode was implanted in the tegmental area which ordinarily evokes the strong escape response. The authors hypothesized that meprobamate tends to inhibit escape and avoidant tendencies. It is interesting that the authors noted that meprobamate appeared to have its most distinctive effect and favored self-stimulation at the cost of an escape reaction in those animals where the electrode was implanted in borderline areas where the stimulation normally evokes ambivalent responses involving both a tendency toward self-stimulation and a tendency toward avoidance.

Weaver and Miya (1961) described the effect of certain ataraxic agents on the activity of mice. In this procedure the spontaneous motor activity of the mice was compared with their performance on a rolling rotor. It was found that the performance on the rolling rotor activity was substantially impaired, but there was no change in the spontaneous motor activity, i.e., the amount of time the animal remained on the rolling rotor activity was reduced by meprobamate without reducing the spontaneous activity of the animals. This was observed at a dosage level 100 mg. per kilogram of body weight, and it is possible that the results were due either to ataxia or incoordination in the animals or to weakening of the animal's struggle to avoid falling from the rotor. Conceivably this result could be ascribed to diminution of the avoidant components of the rotor performance.

A report by Kelleher et al. (1961) described the effect of meprobamate on operant behavior in rats. These investigators found that at dosages which did not approach the neurotoxic level meprobamate had no effect on conditioned bar pressing in rats. Thus it would appear that this report confirms the implication of other reports that meprobamate has no adverse effect on acquired behavior *per se,* particularly, if it has no avoidant component.

Perhaps the most incisively conceived and adequately conducted studies of the effect of meprobamate on avoidant behavior have been described by Ray. In his report (1963) Ray reminds the reader of the possible distinction between escape behavior and acquired avoidant behavior. Ray employed a procedure which involved two identical manipulanda and two different conditioned stimuli. The conditioned stimulus to signal the delivery of a shock was a thousand cycle tone. The shock could be averted by responding to one of the manipulanda. In addition, a five hundred cycle tone was used to signal the delivery for a milk reinforcement upon the response to the reward manipulandum. Data were presented showing that meprobamate had the effect of increasing the latency of the avoidant response without appreciably affecting the response leading to milk reinforcement. Data were presented for five animals, three receiving 90 mg. per kilogram of body weight. It is interesting to note that the avoidant effect of meprobamate was relatively short lived and was not appreciable after the third hour.

In his 1965 report, Ray hypothesized that if a tranquilizer does indeed reduce anxiety then one should make the following prediction: (1) an increase in response latency in avoidance learning (2) an increase in response rate to stimuli which have been paired with stock in a conditioned suppression paradigm (3) an increase in approach responses in the approach-avoidance conflict situations. The data of the 1963 report were used to support the first hypothesis predicting increased latency in avoidance procedures.

The conditioned suppression paradigm required by his second prediction was conducted in the following manner: In the positive training sequence, an auditory stimulus was used as a signal that a lever response would be reinforced by water, and in the suppression sequence the houselights were used as a signal for shock. Turning out the houselights which ordinarily signal shock just prior to the auditory signal for water reinforcement was found to suppress the conditioned response to the auditory stimulus or reinforcement. Meprobamate did not attenuate this conditioned suppression; i.e., under meprobamate administration the suppressive response to the auditory stimulus on the occasion of the flashing of the light which signaled shock continued to interfere with the response to the auditory stimulus.

In the approach-avoidance situation, a flashing light indicated that pressing the bar would deliver milk reinforcement. On some trials a tone preceded and continued through the light flashing sequence. The presence of a tone indicated that the animal would receive a shock for each reinforcement he had received. Thus a conflict trial was one where the flashing light indicating that positive reinforcement was available was accompanied by a tone indicating that the positive reinforcement would be accompanied by a shock. On these trials the animal could avoid both positive reinforcement and shock by refraining from pressing the lever. If he received reinforcement (and he could receive as many as four during the light-flashing sequence), he would receive a corresponding number of shocks. After training the animals received positive reinforcement to the light alone 95% to 100% of the time, but when the light was paired with the tone, they inhibited their response 95% to 100% of the time, thereby avoiding both shock and positive reinforcement. In consequence of meprobamate, there was an increase in the number of responses made in the conflict trials. Some degree of increase was observed for all of the animals for which data were displayed and the effect lasted up to three hours. The dosage varied up to 140 mg. per kilograms of body weight.

Although meprobamate did increase response latencies to shock-paired stimuli without increasing the latencies to the milk-paired stimuli and meprobamate did increase the number of responses in the approach avoidant conflict situation, meprobamate did not increase the number of responses in conditioned suppression situation where the tone signaling the availability of water reinforcement was preceded and accompanied by a light signaling an inevitable shock. It should be noted that in the conditioned suppression paradigm the positive reinforcement was milk or water. Thus it is possible that the difference between these two situations is confounded with difference in the reinforcement. Nevertheless, in two of the three situations described by Ray meprobamate was followed by a reduction in the avoidant behavior.

The attenuating effect on acquired avoidant reactions appears to be confirmed by most pertinent studies. For example, in 1963, Lauener reported an inhibition of conditioned suppression in rats who were treated with meprobamate. The rats were trained to press a bar in order to receive water. This lever-pressing response was suppressed in the animals by introducing a buzzer which had been associated with an unavoidable shock. In the animals treated with meprobamate, the suppression of the lever-pressing response was somewhat attenuated, i.e., the number of lever presses increased under meprobamate medication. This study must be considered concurrently with the report of Ray's study wherein it was indicated that meprobamate had no effect on the conditioned suppression of a response. The distinction between a conditioned avoidant response and a conditioned escape attempt in response to the shock must be observed. In a study of this kind where the buzzer signaled an unavoidable shock, the suppressive effect may be due more to escape reaction to the stimulus than to an anticipatory avoidant response to the conditioning signal.

In 1963, Tanabe examined the pole jumping response as a function of meprobamate dosage. The pole jumping response was an avoidant response that had been conditioned to a buzzer. It was found that as little as 50 mg. per kilogram had an appreciable effect on the pole jumping response. At 120 mg. per kilogram, however, 55% of the total possible conditioned responses were occurring, and at 200 mg. 17% of the possible conditioned avoidant responses continued to occur. Thus it is apparent that meprobamate substantially reduced the conditioned avoidant responses, but in this situation it appeared not to eliminate the response in the dosages ranges employed.

In 1963, Tamura described a conflict study employing adult dogs. These animals had been trained to press a lever in order to activate a buzzer which, in turn, was the signal to lift the lid of the food box in order to obtain food. After this pattern of response was well established, the conflict situation was developed by employing a punishment experience every ten trials. Specifically, on every tenth trial the food box and the floor in front of it were charged so that the animals would receive an electric shock every ten trials. After some experience with this sequence, the dogs reduced the feeding sequence, while other forms of behavior increased. When the deviant somewhat avoidant behaviors were well established, the shock was randomly omitted from the sequence. The bell which had been the signal for the shock was continued for every tenth feeding trial. Under these circumstances, it required from two to three months for the untreated dogs to re-establish their normal food-taking behavior. Meprobamate was found to improve the conflict behavior and increase the feeding activity to a marked degree, however, ataxia was noticed in all dogs. The dosage level ranged from 70 to 100 mg. per kilogram of body weight. It is interesting to note that although meprobamate had the effect of reducing or eliminating conflict behavior, no such effect was observed for chlorpromazine. It is apparent that meprobamate had the effect of diminishing the avoidant aspects of this conflict behavior.

Other studies of this period should be described. One by Marriott and Spencer (1965) used a y-maze in order to study the effect of various drugs on exploratory behavior. It was found that meprobamate was accompanied by increases in exploratory behavior which became statistically significant at 200 mg. per kilograms of body weight.

As some of these reports indicate, particularly Lynch et al. (1960), a diminution of avoidance responses is not invariably observed in consequence of the administration of meprobamate. For example, in 1965 Powell et al. found that meprobamate actually increased the number of avoidant responses among rats who could avoid shock by jumping over a hurdle. As in Ray's suppression paradigm, the conditioned stimulus for the delivery of shock was a flashing light.

There are many reports of studies where the effect of meprobamate on fear-like or so called emotional behavior has been examined. Cole and Wolf reported a conditioned avoidant study in 1966. This study is somewhat distinctive in that it failed to show any effect of meprobamate on the conditioned avoidant response. The apparatus was a plexiglass box with a starting chamber at one end and at the other end a raised platform which the animal could mount in order to escape from an electrically charged floor. The procedure involved sounding a buzzer after the rat was placed in the starting chamber. After five seconds of the signal, the shock was delivered while the buzzer continued. Before the administration of the drug, each animal was screened by placing him in the starting box, exposing him to the shock, and requiring him to perform the escape response within five seconds.

These investigators also examined the effect of meprobamate on fighting behavior. They reported that meprobamate was effective in reducing the conditioned avoidant responses and in reducing the fighting behavior only at those dosages which were neurotoxic, specifically at 255 and 310 mg. per kilogram, respectively. Thus it is apparent that the conditioned avoidant response, as well as fighting behavior, can persist despite meprobamate treatment. It may be noted, however, that prior to each administration of the drug the animal was exposed to one shock trial without the warning buzzer. The influence of this escape trial may be involved in persistence of the avoidant response in the animals receiving meprobamate.

Miscellaneous

A group of miscellaneous, somewhat relevant studies includes a report by Horsley Gantt (1964). This investigation showed that in the classical conditioning of a dog the presentation of a conditioned stimulus for shock was associated with a substantial increase in heart rate. In this situation the presentation of the conditioned stimulus might be construed as eliciting an avoidant response to the anticipated shock. It was shown that meprobamate eliminated the increased heart rate which ordinarily occurred in response to this conditioned stimulus. Is it possible that this may be construed as the elimination of both the avoidant response to the conditioned stimulus and its physiologic accompaniment?

In 1962, Feldman and Lewis reported a study where a jumping apparatus was used to induce an anxious state in rats. In this procedure, the animals were first trained to jump through a window in order to receive food. Subsequently the animals were subjected to an insoluble problem situation in the sense that the windows were interchanged and intermittenly locked in such a way that the animal could be positively reinforced in only fifty per cent of the trials. In this situation the animals assumed a position stereotype, a fixated behavior which persisted in the second stage of training where the problem became soluble by virtue of the fact that one of the windows was a consistently correct choice. In this second stage, it was found that when the correct window appeared on the fixated side, the animals jumped with a short latency. When the incorrect window appeared on the fixated side, the animals continued to jump with some hesitation. It was found that none of a series of tranquilizers, including meprobamate, was effective in eliminating the fixated response. The fixated behavior obviously is not an avoidant response, but it does appear to have a neurotic quality and may be considered to be emotionally toned.

In 1962, Masserman referred to some explorations of the effect of various drugs on experimental neurosis in cats and monkeys. It was reported that tranquilizers, including meprobamate, provided less immediate relief from experimentally induced neurotic or psychotic behavior than alcohol or barbiturates. The exact nature of the procedures employed is not indicated, and it is not possible to assess the importance of any absolute effects produced by any of the substances.

Janssen et al. (1963) described the effect of several drugs, including analgesics, on the tail withdrawal reflex in rats. They reported that meprobamate at 160 mg. per kilogram of body weight had no effect on the tail withdrawal reflex. Thus we are reminded that the action of meprobamate is not a consequence of any anesthetic or analgesic effect.

There were several studies which explored the possible effect of meprobamate when administered to pregnant animals. In 1962, Werboff and Havlena described the postnatal behavioral effects when tranquilizers had been administered to the pregnant rat. In this study the drugs were injected for a period of four successive days, and the dosages were 1 mg. per kilogram of reserpine, 6 mg. per kilogram of chlorpromazine, and 60 mg. per kilogram of meprobamate. The offspring were tested on measures of activity, emotionality, and audiogenic seizure susceptibility.

Relative to a control group, all drugs resulted in a reduced activity as measured by the inclined plane test. Emotionality was measured by the open field test. In the reserpine and meprobamate groups, the amount of exploration was reduced. Whether this reflects a greater emotionality or reduced activity is not certain. The measure of seizure susceptibility showed that the drug groups had less seizure susceptibility and shorter seizures than the control group. In general, the direction of the behavioral consequence of these three drugs on progeny is the same and suggests less activity and emotionality and a reduced susceptibility to audiogenic seizures.

The effect of drugs, such as meprobamate, on progeny is far from clear. For example, in 1964, Caldwell and Spille reported a study where pregnant females throughout their gestation and lactation received daily administrations of meprobamate. Four groups were involved, one receiving placebo, one receiving 32 mg. per kilogram, another 64 mg. per kilogram, and the fourth 128 mg. per kilogram per day. The administration was oral via stomach tube. The female progeny of the meprobamate-treated mothers learned a t-maze in fewer trials than the controls. No such trend was apparent for the males.

In 1965, Hoffeld and Webster examined the effect of injecting tranquilizing drugs during pregnancy. The offspring were examined from the standpoint of weight, performance in maze learning, and conditioned avoidant behavior. In general, there were no differences between drugs, but there were some significant interactions between drug effect and stage of pregnancy. The implications of these data are not clear, but they appear not to provide any indication of an adverse effect with the various drugs employed which included meprobamate, reserpine, and chlorpromazine. There was a trend to indicate that chlorpromazine could have an adverse effect on maze learning.

In 1964, Kletzkin and others examined the postnatal effects of meprobamate injected into the pregnant rat. They examined body weight and maze learning in order to confirm an earlier report of Werboff and Kesner (1963) who found that meprobamate administration to pregnant females resulted in progeny that were of lighter weight and poorer maze learning ability than controls. The report of Kletzkin et al. (1964) failed to confirm the findings of Werboff and Kesner (1963) and did not indicate any postnatal behavioral effects of meprobamate injection into the pregnant female.

Chapter III

STRESS RESPONSES AMONG NORMALS

The very substantial literature that has been generated by investigators examining the effects of meprobamate and related compounds on normal human subjects is strikingly uninformative. The published reports explore virtually every aspect of cognitive and perceptual-motor performance, and the consequences of meprobamate on normal performance appear to be of little practical significance, particularly at dosages within the range of recommended therapeutic use. In some studies slowing or impairment was observed, but it appears to be consistent with the mildly sedating effect of meprobamate and appears to be of little theoretical interest or practical consequence. Of greater interest is the fact that some enhancements of performance have been observed in stress-like situations where the ameliorating, therapeutic effects of meprobamate may be construed as protecting the subject from stress or distracting influences.

The possibility that meprobamate may protect the normal subject from situational stress or circumstances which could detract from his performance is illustrated by a few sound studies. The general quality of these experimental effects appears to be consistent with the effects which may be found to accompany therapeutic use.

In 1960, Uhr and Miller reported the use of elaborately contrived stress experiences to examine the effect of meprobamate on paid volunteer subjects in a Michigan prison. The possible consequences of meprobamate were gauged in terms of a comprehensive battery of psychological procedures which included measures of galvanic skin resistance, various kinds of cognitive-perceptual-psychomotor tests, and subjective reports. The only measure which clearly distinguished meprobamate from placebo was the galvanic skin response which showed a higher skin resistance for the meprobamate-treated subjects. Under meprobamate this reduced autonomic response was accompanied by subjective reports of calmness and relaxation. It was noted that this finding confirmed the work of Laties (1959) who had reported that meprobamate was associated with relatively high levels of skin resistance, and thus it would appear that at least some aspects of the physiologic response to a threatening stress situation may be diminished by the use of meprobamate. It is interesting to note that in the Uhr and Miller experiment (1960) the stress situation comprised numerous and conspicuous elements of threat, and although pain in the form of shock was experienced, restraint and threats, both verbal and sensory (spark gaps, air blasts, and noise), were repeated in various treatment sequences.

The possible effects of meprobamate on the physiological accompaniments of stress are further explored by Frankenhaeuser and Kareby (1962). In this report the dependent variable was the urinary excretion of catecholamines, particularly epinephrine and norepinephrine. The sample comprised a group of 20 medical students, half of whom received placebo an hour and fifteen minutes before the experimental stress and half of whom received 800 mg. of meprobamate; double blind conditions were observed. Prior to the stress trial, baseline values had been established for epinephrine and norepinephrine. During the experiment, urine was collected at the end of each 40 minute period. The experimental procedure comprised three periods: an anticipation period in which the subject was introduced to the test materials with the instructions that these would be used later; a stress period in which the subjects' use of the performance test material was under unfriendly coercion and subject to critical, denigrating evaluation regardless of its quality; and a post-test period in which the subject was interviewed about his feelings and in which the general nature of the procedures, including the reason for his stressful experience, was explained. From the standpoint of the catecholamine excretion, epinephrine increased during the anticipation period and reached a maximum during the stress period. Although the epinephrine output was greater in the placebo group than in the meprobamate group, the difference was not significant. The difference between the two groups in norepinephrine excretion was marked and highly significant statistically for both the anticipation and the stress periods. The post-test period revealed no significant differences in norepinephrine excretion. It may be noted also that self-ratings were made during the successive periods of the experiment and that the placebo group showed a significant increase in extra and intra punitive ratings during the stress periods, while no such change was found for the meprobamate group. It is interesting that meprobamate tended to suppress the excretion of norepinephrine in the anticipatory, as well as in the stress period.

Berger (1957;1960) has designated meprobamate as a central relaxant distinguishable from autonomic suppressants. In this context, the reports by Uhr and Miller (1960) and by Frankenhaeuser and Kareby (1962) assume an interesting position. Although meprobamate need not have a primary effect on the autonomic nervous system as a means of producing therapeutic benefit, it appears that meprobamate is effective in stress situations, particularly when the stress has an anticipatory component, and that associated with this reduced susceptibility to stress situations are reductions in certain aspects of autonomic activity. Conceivably, the apparent autonomic sensitivity to meprobamate may be a function of the nature and chronicity of the stress experienced during the period of medication. It is possible that the acute situational stress experienced by these normal subjects has autonomic accompaniments which are more sensitive to meprobamate than the autonomic accompaniments of the relatively chronic stress experienced by patients who are seeking therapeutic relief.

In 1958, Holliday et al. described a study of the effect of stress upon the pursuit rotor performance of dental students. Stress was in the form of randomly interspersed noise, air blasts, and finger shock. Each of four groups of ten subjects was assigned on a double blind basis to a different pre-task medication. Under chlorpromazine, pentobarbital, and placebo there was a disruption of performance. Under meprobamate, however, there was a continued increase in quality of performance. Since meprobamate is not considered to be an analgesic, its effect presumably was not a result of diminishing the discomfort *per se*. Perhaps meprobamate reduced the detracting anticipatory response to the expected punishment.

In 1964, Uhr et al. reported a study of 12 college students who participated in a double blind, crossover procedure wherein meprobamate (1600 mg. in a single dose) was compared with placebo. The dependent variable was performance on a continuous attention task. The performance period was interspersed with periods of shock, and the attention score was studied as a function of whether performance was during a shock or nonshock period, whether the subject had a high or a low anxiety score on an inventory, and whether he received meprobamate or placebo. Both the preperformance anxiety score and the treatment variables were significantly related with the total performance. The subjects receiving meprobamate performed better than the placebo subjects, thus implying that meprobamate reduced the possible disruptive effects of anxiety. The authors believe that the anticipation of shock may have been the significant anxiety-arousing factor.

In 1963, Di Mascio described the effect of meprobamate on competitive paired associates learning. His procedures involved the learning of pairs of words arranged in such a manner that there were strong pre-established associations between members of contiguous pairs. Thus there were pre-established interfering associations within the series. The experiment involved several different drugs, including meprobamate at two different dosage levels, 800 mg. and 400 mg. At the higher dosage level, the meprobamate group required significantly fewer trials to learn the pairs of words than did the placebo group. Apparently there was some interaction between response to meprobamate and the general level of anxiety as indicated by an inventory. Specifically, there was a tendency, significant at the 0.10 level, for the subjects with the high premedication anxiety scores to benefit more from meprobamate than those with low anxiety scores. Nevertheless, there were no associations involving changes in the subjects' self-rating of anxiety, but the author discounts this by pointing to the insensitivity of the self-rating scale for anxiety.

The theoretical explanation for the effect of meprobamate was expressed in terms of a reduction of anxiety, but no explanation was offered for an association between the presumed reduction in anxiety and the weakening or suppression of previously established competing inter-serial association. Di Mascio noted that his findings were consistent with those of Bernstein and Dorfman (1959) who had used a different basis for organizing competitive paired associates in their demonstration of the efficacy of meprobamate (1200 mg.) in facilitating the learning of competitive paired associates.

In 1966, Margolis showed that meprobamate could facilitate learning by reducing the associative interference of earlier learning. In this experiment a different response was learned to each of six different stimulus words. Subsequently, the subject was required to re-associate these responses to the stimulus words by forming pairs different from those originally learned. Part of the group learned the competing associations under 400 mg. of meprobamate, while the others learned the associations under placebo. As expected, the placebo group had greater difficulty learning the second competing associations than they did in learning the original associations. The meprobamate group, in contrast, had no more difficulty learning the competing associations than in learning the original associations.

Margolis does not explicitly involve the concept of anxiety in the apparent reduction of associative interference following the ingestion of meprobamate. It is possible that both Di Mascio and Margolis may have overlooked the anxiety arousal implicit in a situation where the subject must struggle to learn new associations in the presence of established competing associations which would tend to express themselves in the form of obtrusive errors. Regardless of whether this situation is technically acceptable as an instance of anxiety, it is obviously a stress situation in which the individual struggles for a correct response in the presence of a competing inclination which has its origins within the subject. Thus at the very least, an internal struggle due to two competing responses is inevitable. It is possible that the contribution of meprobamate to this type of learning situation is due to the reduction of situational anxiety which accompanies the anticipation of probable error, and the effect may not be dependent upon a reduction of some general, possibly characteristic level of anxiety.

Thus it appears that meprobamate may reduce effects of situational stress in normals. Stress effects modified by meprobamate in the foregoing reports include psychogalvanic skin response, the excretion of norepinephrine, impaired hand-eye coordination when anticipating shock, impaired attention when anticipating shock, and associative interference in paired associate learning.

It would be premature to conclude that these possible effects of meprobamate on stress responses are invariable or even highly probable. Negative results are somewhat less likely to get into the literature than positive results, and this may explain the absence of clearcut negative results in the present brief review. Stress itself is not an objectively definable factor, and it should be noted that most tasks have elements of stress. Nevertheless, in those many studies where stress was not an explicit component of the performance situation, absolute or relative improvement was occasionally noted but was not a usual accompaniment of meprobamate medication, and in some studies a modest but statistically significant loss was reported. Whether such losses should be ascribed to the slowing or sedating effect of meprobamate or whether these were situations where meprobamate had no ameliorating effect on the stress implicit in the task is debatable. The results reviewed here are sufficient, however, to indicate that meprobamate can have a suppressant effect on the response to stress in normal subjects, particularly in those situations designed to show the effect of meprobamate on stress reactions.

Chapter IV

A PRAGMATIC THEORY
OF MEPROBAMATE EFFECTS

Meprobamate has long been known as an interneuronal blocking agent with anticonvulsant properties, as a central relaxant, and as a mild tranquilizer which may be safely used in the amelioration of anxiety and tension. Nevertheless, certain questions relevant to its optimal use remain unanswered. Specifically, its clinical effects have never been conceptualized in a way to permit a prediction of those particular individuals who will respond with the desired symptomatic modifications and of those individuals whose symptoms may remain relatively unaffected.

During the fourteen years which have followed the introduction of meprobamate, a most substantial literature has developed describing the response of laboratory animals, normal human subjects, medical patients, and psychiatric and behavioral patients. This literature is sufficiently voluminous to justify a search for unifying trends. It was hoped that such trends might lead to inferences which could provide an incisive, behaviorally pertinent conceptualization of the clinical effects of meprobamate, inferences which could be used as the basis for deducing the probable consequences of meprobamate medication in various types of situations. Such deductions, if confirmable, would provide a basis for the predictive identification of those individuals who might or might not be expected to respond to meprobamate in the desired manner.

In a cursory search for recurrent trends, some of the available literature was scrutinized. A primary cue was provided by the animal work which indicated that meprobamate might suppress conditioned avoidant responses. Somewhat commensurate indications were found in work

33

with human subjects suggesting further that meprobamate might have a selectively inhibitory influence on avoidant behavior. These implications, together with clinical observations and a modest number of clinical reports already known to the writer, led to the inference that, in addition to its interneuronal blocking function, meprobamate weakens avoidant responses, possibly by interfering with the acquired anticipatory response to pain and other ordinarily adversive experiences. The effect is not conceived to be one which interferes with primary fear or with pain *per se*, but one which may interfere with the response to the acquired anticipation of pain, either psychic or sensory.

This inference leads to several working generalizations applicable to the clinical use of meprobamate:

1. Meprobamate would be expected to ameliorate behavioral difficulties by reducing abient responses or reactions based on unpleasant anticipations.

2. Meprobamate would not be expected to ameliorate behavioral difficulties involving adient responses or reactions expressive of hostile impulses, sensually gratifying impulses, or responses generated or sustained by positive reinforcement, i.e., robbery, excessive eating, sexual behavior, assaultive acts, or symptomatic aberrations sustained by secondary gains.

3. On this premise, there would be no reason for expecting motor, perceptual, or cognitive responses, including knowledge or memory *per se* of experiences (whether pleasant or unpleasant), to be impaired by meprobamate.

4. Exceptions to these generalizations could occur in situations where the primary interneuronal blocking effect of meprobamate or where side reactions to meprobamate (e.g., possible drowsiness or hypotension) would either obscure or simulate the ordinary inhibitions of avoidant responses.

When these generalizations are applied to common clinical problems, several interesting and specific deductions may be made:

1. When tension may be regarded as involving an anticipatory response to a real or fantasied unpleasant situation, a drug such as meprobamate which suppresses the avoidant struggle (even when it is implicit and symbolic in nature) would be expected to have an ameliorating effect.

2. To the extent that anxiety may be regarded as a more or less unconscious response to a situation that threatens the defenses of the ego, the avoidant components of anxiety must be acknowledged. If meprobamate can diminish the strength of intropsychic avoidant responses, it can be expected to diminish the severity of anxiety, both as a subjective experience and as a symptom-generating condition.

3. Somatic complaints which have a purely hysterical origin and involve important secondary gains would not be predicted to respond to meprobamate.

4. Somatic complaints which are an expression of a strong avoidant response, such as the vomiting of a woman involved in an undesired pregnancy, would be expected to diminish in response to meprobamate (unless the vomiting procured important secondary gains, such as special attention or relief from duties).

5. To the extent that the suspicion and fear of a paranoid patient may be a projective expression of hostile impulses, meprobamate would not be predicted to be efficacious in reducing paranoid fear.

6. Whether depressive symptoms would respond to meprobamate would depend upon their significance. To the extent that the symptoms are used by the patient to control others or to justify or maintain his own role or pattern of interpersonal behavior, the depression is not primarily an avoidant response, regardless of how piteously the patient protests to the contrary. In these situations, meprobamate would not be expected to be an effective treatment.

7. Where the depressive symptoms have no manipulative or role-sustaining function and are a direct avoidant response to a threat, whether real or fantasied, meprobamate would be expected to ameliorate the avoidant or unpleasant anticipatory components of the dysphoric state.

8. To the extent that delusions and hallucinations are expressive of or generated by impulse reactions, particularly hostile or erotic reactions, meprobamate would be expected to be ineffectual.

9. Those disciplinary problems that are based upon an anticipa-

tion of disapproval, blame, punishment, or pain may involve avoidant features that could be reduced by meprobamate.

10. Obsessive ruminations or compulsive acts generated by hostile or erotic impulses would not be responsive to meprobamate medication.

11. Obsessive or compulsive acts that are symbolic avoidant gestures or fantasies would be expected to ameliorate in response to meprobamate.

12. Although meprobamate is reported to have anticonvulsant qualities *per se,* it would be predicted that meprobamate would be of benefit to persons whose behavior is distorted by fearful anticipation of convulsions. Meprobamate would be expected also to benefit persons whose convulsive attacks appear to be precipitated by threatening or distasteful situations, particularly some of the petit mal patients in whom the minute seizures appear to serve as a denial of or as an escape from threatening pressures.

13. Meprobamate would be expected to be helpful in the treatment of geriatric patients who are struggling to avoid death in their sleep or some fatal attack or seizure and as a consequence are restless, apprehensive, fearful of finding themselves helpless, fearful of being left alone at night, and whose insomnia may represent a fear of sleep and all it symbolizes.

14. Meprobamate would be expected to benefit insomniacs who are struggling with the fear that they won't be able to sleep or won't be able to meet the requirements of the coming day.

15. Meprobamate would not be expected to act as an analgesic or to reduce current sensory pain.

16. Meprobamate would be expected to help persons who are anticipating pain, physical threat, or discomfort, such as dental patients or surgical patients.

17. In general, persons who anticipate an unpleasant experience and whose behavior in consequence becomes disruptively avoidant may be helped by meprobamate. Illustrations would include students who have difficulty in reciting in a threatening situation and who go blank or whose performance is aborted in an important examination.

18. In general, meprobamate may help to prevent the disruptive or

paralyzing panic-like responses which occur in situations where the avoidant response is strong.

19. Because meprobamate reduces avoidant responses, it would be subject to overdose by the patient. Overdosage could occur among housewives who dislike their domestic role and struggle without avail in their avoidant reactions to an obdurate reality, or it could occur among persons who have suicidal motivations and seek to avoid the challenge of life or seek to escape from the anxiety which may accompany the anticipation of their own demise.

20. It is possible also that meprobamate could lead to acting out behavior among persons whose expressive impulses had been deterred by fear.

21. To the extent that meprobamate reduces tension and anxiety which are associated with avoidant tendencies, the physiologic correlates of tension and anxiety would be reduced correspondingly.

22. Resistance to circumstances, activities, or verbalizations which are associated primarily with an acquired avoidant reaction would be reduced under meprobamate medication so that patients could be more cooperative and less resistant.

Although some of these hypotheses provide predictions concerning the possible efficacy of meprobamate for the amelioration of explicit symptomatic manifestations, in several instances their predictive value relies upon some understanding of the motivational basis of the symptoms. For example, whether symptoms such as resistance and somatic complaints would be expected to respond to meprobamate medication would depend upon whether the symptoms were an expression of a primarily avoidant motivational disposition.

In attempting to apply the hypotheses predictively, considerable uncertainty and prognostic error are inherent in the fact that symptoms may be in the service of a motivational complex in which some of the motivational components may be avoidant, while others are expressive or assertive. Thus in many situations meprobamate could be partially effective in the sense that it would be expected to reduce the avoidant components, but at the same time not fully or even significantly effective because of expressive or assertive components which are sufficient to sustain the symptom. This is but another illustration of the conceptual and investigational difficulties encountered in the study of behaviors which are overdetermined in the sense that they are a consequence of several causes, each of which is sufficient by itself.

In order to examine the possible pertinence of the hypotheses, the literature was scanned for all available reports of controlled clinical studies which could be examined from the standpoint of any congruence between one or more of the hypotheses and the reported consequences of meprobamate medication. If the hypotheses are well founded, the reports of therapeutic efficacy should tend to be consistent with the provisions of the hypotheses, and the reports of therapeutic failure should describe situations in which no therapeutic gain could be anticipated from the hypotheses.

It must be recognized that such *ex post facto* applications of the predictive hypotheses can involve important elements of subjectivity, and interpretive error could work either to confirm or to discredit the pertinent hypothesis. Even where the consequences of treatment are reported in such an explicit manner that interpretive errors are improbable, the possibility remains that the direct consequences of treatment may, in some applications, fail to provide a proper clue to the validity of the hypotheses. This is because the causes of the behavior in question involve unknown motivational determiners, and the avoidance motive may be only a minor part of the predisposing complex of causes.

Chapter V

CONTROLLED STUDIES OF
THERAPEUTIC EFFECT

The premise that meprobamate ameliorates behavioral difficulties by reducing acquired avoidant reactions may illuminate the conditions under which and the individuals for whom meprobamate is an effective medication. In order to pursue this possibility, the present chapter provides a review of the controlled clinical studies which describe a therapeutic consequence of meprobamate medication. Any correspondence between the conditions under which meprobamate was reported to be efficacious and the various conditions hypothesized in the foregoing list of deductive statements will be noted in the course of the review. In this way some estimate may be formed of the value of these hypotheses as an aid in refining our predictions of the individuals and circumstances for which meprobamate treatment may be effective.

This review is limited to those studies which involve the principle of controlled comparisons and which describe therapeutic effects with sufficient clarity to make replication possible. The material is organized on the basis of several substantive topics pertinent to familiar areas of clinical application.

Geriatric Patients

In the reports published prior to 1960, three controlled or comparative studies based on geriatric patients revealed clear indication of beneficial effect. In a 1957 study undertaken by Settel for the purpose of examining the efficacy of phenaglycodol for the treatment of geriatric patients, meprobamate was used in a crossover comparison. The total sample of 67 aged patients included 23 who were in a nursing home and described as psychotic and severely agitated. The remaining 44 were ambulatory with the typical anxiety, tension, organic complaint syndrome of the aged. Phenaglycodol was administered as the primary and initial treatment. Excellent or good responses were found among most of the ambulatory patients and for about half of the hospitalized patients. During the course of treatment, for 30 of the patients meprobamate was substituted for a period of 10 weeks and then the patients were returned to phenaglycodol. This substitution was made without the awareness of the nursing personnel or the responsible member of the family who, at two-week intervals, provided standard assessment ratings. No appreciable change in reaction or behavior was reported for the 10 inpatients and 20 ambulatory patients who were involved in the meprobamate substitution, nevertheless these patients were observed to be somewhat sleepier during their waking hours while on meprobamate than on phenaglycodol.

In a similar manner placebo also was substituted for phenaglycodol for 20 of the ambulatory patients who had been reacting favorably. Recurrence of symptoms was described for 18 of these 20 placebo patients within 48 hours. Restlessness, agitation, and anxiety returned to pretreatment levels within a week. Upon resumption of phenaglycodol, control was regained in three or four days.

On the basis of this account, it would appear that both meprobamate and phenaglycodol are effective in the management of senile agitation, restlessness, and anxiety and that this benefit was not sustained when placebo was substituted for the active medication. These findings correspond with the requirements of hypotheses 1 and 2 which describe some of the avoidant struggle which can be seen in the distress of senile patients.

The effectiveness of meprobamate in the management of senile patients was indicated also in a Scandinavian report by Jensen et al. (1957). In this crossover study, there were 17 senile patients who were examined on a double blind basis. The initial treatment was either meprobamate or placebo with a beginning dosage regimen of $1 + 1 + 2$ 400 mg. tablets per day; the last two were sleeping tablets. After 10 to 14 days of treatment the medications were exchanged. Twelve of the 13 patients were reported to have responded favorably while on meprobamate, but only four of the 13 responded favorably to placebo. Although the exact observations that provided the judgment of "improved" were not indicated, it is clear that the difference is statistically significant at a high level. The authors commented that the primary effect of meprobamate was improved sleep at night, an effect which is anticipated by the provisions of hypothesis 13. It was specified that with few exceptions the patients were able to get along without hypnotics. Prior to and subsequent to the meprobamate treatment, however, large doses of scopolamine, morphine, or hypnophen had been used. During the day the effect of meprobamate was less pronounced. Meprobamate was not observed to affect the confusion, dementia, or paranoia apparent in some of these patients.

The efficacy of meprobamate in treating senile patients is indicated also in a study of meprobamate withdrawal by Boyd et al. (1958). Sixty geriatric patients were treated with meprobamate, and 30 received an indistinguishable placebo under double blind conditions. After 8 weeks of treatment at a 1200 mg. per day level, placebo was substituted for meprobamate, and the patients were observed for any withdrawal symptoms for an additional period of two weeks. Although there were two patients who became restless after meprobamate was stopped, such symptoms were found in the placebo group as well, and it was concluded that appreciable withdrawal symptoms could not be expected following the use of meprobamate at this dosage level (400 mg. three times per day). This was found to be a therapeutically effective dosage level, however; specifically, 64% of the patients receiving meprobamate reported that they slept better at night, while only 28% of the placebo patients reported improvement, a finding consistent with hypothesis 13.

The possibility that even small doses of meprobamate may have appreciable effects in the aged is indicated in a report by Krugman et al. (1960) who compared 400 mg. daily doses of meprobamate with 5mg. of d-amphetamine and 5 mg. of an inactive placebo. There were 12, 10, and 9 patients in the respective treatment groups; these patients ranged in age from 59 to 83 years and were in a Veterans Administration domiciliary. They were tested one hour after receiving the medication. The criteria of change included several measures of intellectual performance and the Clyde Mood Scale. Although there were no indications that performance was modified by medication, there were changes in the clear thinking portion of the Clyde Mood Scale, an indication of how clearly the individual feels he is thinking but not an assessment of the clarity of thinking *per se*. No effect on performance is hypothesized for meprobamate, nor was any increase in the subjective experience of clear thinking specifically anticipated. It is possible that the subjective feeling of clear thinking may be associated with some reduction of tension and anxiety in a way related to hypotheses 1 or 17. According to this measure, the patients on d-amphetamine were most affected in the sense that they felt less alert and less able to concentrate than the placebo patients. The meprobamate patients, although significantly more affected than the placebo patients, did not experience nearly as much of this subjective effect as the d-amphetamine patients.

A later report by Exton-Smith et al. (1963) confirmed the measurable effect of low doses of meprobamate in the treatment of elderly patients. The sample comprised 65 females who ranged in age from 59 to 93 years and who were recent admissions to a geriatric unit. Four drugs were compared under double blind conditions: amobarbital (200 mg.) dichloralphenazone (1300 mg.), chlorpromazine (50 mg.), and meprobamate (800 mg.). These four drugs and a lactose placebo were given one night each to each patient. The medications were administered on successive nights through a five-day period. The medication was administered at 9:15 in the evening, and the results were assessed later at 10:30 and at hourly intervals until 5:30 on the following morning. At 8:00 A.M. the patient was asked about her night's rest. Sequential analyses based on both the nurse's observations and the patients' reports were used. Both dichloralphenazone and meprobamate were discriminated favorably by the patients to a significant degree. This result for meprobamate is anticipated by hypothesis 13. Significant distinctions between the other two drugs and placebo did not emerge. The authors suggest that freedom from morning hangover contributed to the patients' judgment of effectiveness.

Stutterers

There are reports indicating that meprobamate can be effective in the treatment of persons who stutter. Stutterers may be observed to suffer a double handicap: first, the communication difficulty implicit in stuttering itself; and second, the accompanying tension and anxiety which may intensify the stuttering. Holliday (1959) reported a study based on a selected group of 20 male stutterers. The subjects, who ranged in age from 21–38 years, were assigned at random to either placebo or meprobamate (800 mg. t.i.d.), and the treatment and assessments were conducted on a double blind basis. The inquiry followed a pretesting-posttesting design with the posttesting after three weeks of medication. The testing required that each subject read a standard passage of 200 words before a microphone. Although he was alone at the time, his voice was recorded and he was observed through a one-way mirror. The three variables for analysis included the number of words in which there was any hesitation or irregularity, the average duration of any blocking time occasioned by a stuttering response to a word, and the degree of physical involvement or muscular tension as judged by the unseen speech therapist observers. These observations were rated on a standard scale comprising 17 items referring to various indications of muscular tension or physical struggle. Correlations between the ratings of the two judges showed the scale to be acceptably reliable.

It was found that all but one of the patients in the meprobamate group showed a reduction in the physical tension total score, and none of them showed a gain. In the placebo group, however, only six showed a reduction, and four showed a gain in tension. The average change in the meprobamate group was statistically significant, but there was no significant reduction in the placebo group. Although this report provided no indication that meprobamate differentially reduced stuttering *per se,* it was found to contribute to a reduction in apparent tension, a result which is consistent with hypothesis 1.

In the same year (1959), Di Carlo et al. described a study based upon a sample of 30 stutterers. They ranged in age from 15–45 years, and during the course of the inquiry, all other therapy was held in abeyance. The subjects were seen once a week for a period of six weeks. The sample was divided into three subgroups: ten received meprobamate, ten placebo, and ten received no medication. Before treatment began and at the end of each week, a 500 word passage was read and recorded. The recordings were scored independently by the experimenter and the speech therapist. The treatment and the handling of the data were conducted on a double blind basis. The dosage was graduated with 600 mg. per day being administered the first week, 1200 mg. the second week, 1600 mg. the third week, and 2000 mg. the fourth week. The meprobamate group showed a reduction in the mean number of stuttered moments and when interviewed these individuals said they felt more relaxed. No such improvements were apparent for the placebo or the no-medication groups. The trend toward reduction was considered to be statistically significant in the meprobamate group. This kind of finding may be regarded as consistent with hypotheses 1, 2, 17, or 18.

Thus the Di Carlo et al. study (1959) confirms the positive indications of the Holliday study (1959) and contributes to a conclusion that meprobamate may be useful in work with stutterers. It may be noted, however, that the two studies are not exactly mutually confirmatory because Holliday found a reduction in tension without a reduction in the number of stuttering vocalizations, while Di Carlo et al., who did not study tension independently, did find a tendency to reduction in the amount of stuttering *per se*. When asked about their subjective responses, nine of the subjects in the Di Carlo meprobamate group reported that they were more relaxed, while only 2 in the placebo group reported that they were more relaxed. Although Holliday and Di Carlo assessed *de facto* tension on a different basis, they both presented trends indicating that stutterers treated with meprobamate may experience a reduction in tension.

Other Nonpsychiatric Patients

There were other reports indicating that meprobamate may be used efficaciously with nonpsychiatric patients. In 1959, Boyd et al. described a study which provided a comparison of meprobamate with placebo in the treatment of hypertensive patients, many of whom were elderly. Fifty-seven received meprobamate and 29 placebo. After 8 weeks of meprobamate treatment, placebo was substituted for an additional 5 weeks. Thus there were two controls, a placebo group control and a placebo cross-over control. The dosage was 1200 mg. daily, and the criterion was change in blood pressure. The effects of meprobamate on blood pressure were described as rapid and occurred during the first day in most cases. There was a decrease in both the placebo and meprobamate groups, an average decrement of 8.5 mm Hg. for the controls and 13 mm Hg. for the meprobamate group. Although these drops were statistically significant and occurred in both sexes, the drop was greater in the meprobamate group than in the placebo group. The decrement in the meprobamate group was not significantly greater than the decrement in the placebo group. Nevertheless, when placebo was substituted for meprobamate, the blood pressure tended to rise to the pretreatment level. This slight hypotensive effect may be no more than the usual direct physiologic effect of tranquilizing medication. To some degree, however, it may represent a correlate of reduced anxiety, such as described in hypothesis 21.

It was possible also for these authors to compare the placebo and meprobamate effects for a subgroup of patients whose systolic blood pressure was under 140 mm. It was found that nine of 18 subjects in the placebo group showed a drop; the average fall for the placebo group was 13 mm. For the meprobamate group, the drop was 25 mm. with the decrement occurring in 24 of 31 patients. Both these decrements were found to be statistically significant, and the decrement in the meprobamate group was significantly greater than the decrement in the placebo group.

It may be observed that there were no withdrawal symptoms when placebo was substituted for meprobamate, a finding consistent with the results of the Boyd et al. (1958) investigation. Similar side effects were found in both the meprobamate and the placebo groups with the exception that somnolence and sudden falls were more prevalent among the meprobamate group than among the placebo group.

Friedman (1957) has reported a study of the use of meprobamate in treating patients who complained of frequent headaches. The patients were not hospitalized and ranged in age from 21–65 years. The emphasis was prophylactic, and the relief of symptoms in any given attack was not the focus. About half of the study was described as double blind. Patients were started on 1200 mg. per day, but the dosage reached as high as 4000 mg. and the average was described as 1600 mg. The treatment was continued from 3 to 14 months, with an initial treatment period of 4 weeks. Of the 210 patients receiving meprobamate, 150 were described as having tension headaches and 50 had migraine. Improvement was noted in 67% of the tension headaches and in 55% of the migraines. Thus the efficacy of meprobamate for the reduction of tension receives further confirmation. This result appears to be consistent with several hypotheses, particularly 1, 4, and 21.

Eisenberg (1957) described the use of meprobamate in the treatment of allergic patients who exhibited undue anxiety or tension or who failed to respond to usual allergy treatment. The sample comprised 83 adults who were treated over the course of 6 weeks according to the following treatment substitution schedule:

    —for the first two weeks, meprobamate (Miltown) at a dosage of
        1600 mg. per day
    —for the next two weeks, mephenesin at 2000 mg. per day
    —for the last two weeks, meprobamate (Equanil) 1600 mg. per day

Definite improvement of allergic symptoms was reported for 32 or 39%
of the patients while on meprobamate (Equanil). Patients remarked on
the relaxing and sedative effects of meprobamate and the relief of
anxiety and tension. These consequences of treatment appear to be consistent with the provisions of hypotheses 2, 4, and 21. Treatment was
discontinued for several patients because of side effects, including
angioneurotic edema of the face and neck. No signs of addiction occurred.

Meprobamate has been used as a preanesthetic medication by Eger
and Keasling (1959). A double blind procedure was followed in a comparison of meprobamate (400 g.), pentobarbital (40 mg.), and a
lactose placebo. These medications were administed the afternoon prior
to the morning of surgery, the evening before surgery, and one hour
before the scheduled anesthetic. Increasingly greater amounts were given
on the successive dosages on the basis of the age and weight of the
patient. The maximum preoperative dosage was 160 mg. pentobarbital
and 1600 mg. meprobamate. A standard procedure was employed in
evaluating the patients. This included ratings with respect to apprehension and cooperation, and the patient was also asked a standard set of
questions shortly before anesthesia was administered. When asked
whether they had a good night's sleep, 82% of the meprobamate and
79% of the pentobarbital group were positive, while only 56% of the
placebo group were positive. This was a significant contrast between
medication and placebo. In reply to the question, "Are you comfortable?" there were no significant differences, but when asked, "Are you
worried?" a significant difference was again found between the medication and the placebo group. In addition, the ratings revealed significant
differences in apprehension between the medicated and the placebo
group; this was due to significant increases in the placebo group. This
pattern of effect is consistent with hypotheses 1, 14, and 16. These trends
were marked in the patients under 60 and apparent in patients over 60.
No significant difference was found in patients so deteriorated as to be
described as senile. There were also significant differences in cooperation, with more of the medicated patients becoming cooperative and

fewer uncooperative than in the placebo patients, a result consistent with hypotheses 18 and 22. This pattern was significant only for those patients who were under 60 years of age. The medicated patients were more drowsy than the placebo patients, and there was also a contrast between the two medications, with pentobarbital producing the greater drowsiness. Differences between the two medications were considered to be minor, and they were judged to be equally adequate. The advantage of the medications was generally most apparent among patients under 60 years of age.

There are other reports indicating the value of meprobamate as a preanesthetic medication. For example, Herbring and Wiklund (1960) reported a double blind comparison of Nuncital, meprobamate, and placebo. Nuncital was given on a premedication schedule of 200 mg. the night before the operation and 200 mg. the following morning an hour before the operation. There were 120 cases treated according to this schedule. A comparable group of 75 patients was given 600 mg. meprobamate the night before and 600 mg. the morning before the operation as premedication. In both of these medication programs, patients received from 0.5 to 0.75 mg. atropine as premedication. In this situation, calmness and sedation were considered desirable, and wakefulness and vigilance were not considered to be desirable. In response to inquiry about sleep during the preoperative night, it was found that meprobamate was superior to both Nuncital and placebo, and it was found also that there were fewer requests for additional hypnotics among the meprobamate group than in the Nuncital or placebo groups. These results are consistent with hypotheses 14 and 16. From the standpoint of the patient's condition immediately prior to operation, the condition of the meprobamate patients was considered to be slightly superior to that of the placebo patients, while the Nuncital patients were considered to be less sedated than the placebo patients. The report does not indicate the nature of the data analysis; it appeared from the clinical standpoint, however, that meprobamate may have been slightly more sedating than placebo, while Nuncital was slightly more alerting. Thus the implications of this report are in agreement with implications of the available literature concerning the mild, tranquilizing, relaxing, or sedating effect of meprobamate.

Gruhzit and Lee (1959) described the use of large doses of meprobamate in the treatment of withdrawal symptoms among a sample of 15 hospitalized heroin addicts. A placebo control group was selected at random from an available pool of appropriate patients and treated in a comparable manner with an indistinguishable medication. The dosage regimen was established on the basis of preliminary trials and comprised an initial dose of 400 mg., followed four hours later by 1600 mg., and the subsequent administration of 1200 mg. at four hour intervals during the balance of the five days of withdrawal treatment. The abstinence syndrome was rated with respect to severity, and it was reported that five days of placebo treatment were required to produce the diminution of severity that was observed after one day of meprobamate. Although meprobamate did not appear to affect the respiratory symptoms of wheezing and hoarseness, there was apparent diminution in gastrointestinal complaints. The weight gain was small, but it was significantly greater in the meprobamate group than in the placebo group. Hyperactive tendon reflexes were initially characteristic of both groups. In the placebo group, there was a gradual return to normal during the course of hospitalization, but in the meprobamate group the reflexes became hypoactive within 24 hours, and during the 48 to 72 hour period a patellar reflex could not be elicited in some of the meprobamate patients. In order to explore this phenomenon further a comparable dosage regimen was administered to normal volunteers, all of whom became weak, dizzy, and ataxic. With continued dosage, the ankle and knee reflexes disappeared. All of the volunteers returned to normal within 72 to 96 hours following cessation of the meprobamate.

One patient in the meprobamate group developed withdrawal symptoms of the grand mal type approximately 20 hours after abrupt cessation of medication. The authors suggest that because of this risk gradual diminution would be preferable. The fact that only one withdrawal reaction was observed was ascribed to the short duration of treatment (five days). It may be noted that in addition to the observable benefit experienced by the meprobamate group there were subjective indications of efficacy of the treatment. Specifically, placebo patients noted that they were not as comfortable as other patients and questioned the cause of the difference. Meprobamate patients who had had prior withdrawal experience commented that the period of intense distress was much shorter, i.e., less than two days, than the usual period of suffering and confusion which ordinarily lasted about ten days. Although the study was not conducted in a way to reveal the potential of meprobamate for preventing withdrawal symptoms, it does present a variety of mutually consistent indictions that meprobamate does shorten and ameliorate the withdrawal distress. To the extent that the withdrawal distress is related to the dread of somatic effects and panic over the prospect of being deprived of the drug or exposed to one's own unaided coping devices, the positive results reported here are consistent with some of the hypotheses, particularly 1, 12, 16, 18, and 21.

A 1958 report by Blanc and Gunn-Sechehaye indicated that meprobamate was more efficacious than placebo in reducing nausea and vomiting during pregnancy. Apparently the probability of a favorable response was greater among younger women who were treated earlier in their pregnancy. If women who are vomiting late in pregnancy have secured more secondary gains than those vomiting in early pregnancy, the effect described by these investigators may be interpreted as consistent with the provisions of hypothesis 4.

The use of meprobamate as a hypnotic agent in the treatment of medical patients received confirmation in the 1963 report by Rickels and Bass. In this study, meprobamate was compared with placebo and with six other hypnotic agents. Meprobamate was significantly more effective than placebo, and its effectiveness was found to be midway among the seven hypnotic agents tested. Effectiveness was indicated in terms of the amount of time it took the patient to go to sleep. When effectiveness was assessed in terms of duration of sleep, however, the same comparative pattern was found. Several other indices were employed, all of which showed meprobamate to be superior to placebo and midway in the effective range established for the hypnotics examined. The relevance of meprobamate for insomnia is predicted by hypothesis 14. This pattern of results was not sustained in a comparative group of psychotic patients.

Children

There were several studies illustrating the safe and effective use of meprobamate with children. A report by Litchfield (1957) described the use of meprobamate among pediatric outpatients who were not considered sufficiently disturbed to justify psychiatric referral, but who were sufficiently restless, irritable, aggressive, or tense to become a problem both to themselves and to their families. The study was based on 28 children, five of whom were under four years of age, 16 between 4 and

8, and 8 between 8 and 16. In this oldest group there were three petit mal epileptic patients. Dosage level was adjusted according to the severity of the symptoms and the response of the patients. In the youngest group, 100 mg. in divided dosages was considered to be sufficient. The four-to-eight-year-old group responded well to 400 mg. daily. In general, meprobamate was found to be effective in treating symptoms of irritability, sleeplessness, and restlessness. These results are consistent with the provisions of hypotheses 1, 9, 12, and 14. It was noted that the petit mal patients became less irritable also and that the medication stabilized the emotional upsets of the older children. In a control group of 16 placebo patients, no relief was observed for children showing comparable symptoms. The treatment was described as essentially nontoxic and effective in relaxing children without any resultant retardation in mental ability.

Linzenich (1958) described the use of meprobamate as an aid in assisting children to adjust to pediatric hospitalization. The interest in meprobamate was stimulated by dissatisfaction with the distortions and impairments of behavior which accompany the use of typical sedatives.

The sample of 82 children was divided into two groups of equal size. One of them received meprobamate, and the other received placebo during the first 12 hours of hospitalization. During the succeeding six days, the continuing record of the child's behavior was made with special emphasis on disposition. The study was conducted under double blind conditions. Positive responses were reported for 81% of the meprobamate group and 49% of the placebo group, a finding consistent with the provisions of hypotheses 9 and 22. The difference in the proportion of favorable responses was described as statistically significant. The investigator was willing to generalize his results to all ages and added conviction to his report of efficacy by observing that recurrence of symptoms occurred when the treatment period was short, but that the symptoms would remit again when the treatment was resumed.

Evidence of untoward response among children receiving unusually high dosage levels was presented in a report by Rawitt (1959). In his double blind crossover study, 40 boys with substantial psychiatric disorders were studied over a period of 100 days. The patients ranged from 10–16 years of age, and the largest groups were conduct disturbances (11 patients) and childhood schizophrenia (15 patients).

The study began with 20 boys on meprobamate and 20 on placebo.

After 30 days the treatments were switched. The medication was discontinued on the 60th day, but the patients were observed for the ensuing 40 days. Treatment began for all patients at 1200 mg. per day. This dosage was increased by one 400 mg. tablet t.i.d. at the end of every five days. This pattern of increment was continued until some change was observed. In 20 days 14 of the boys were receiving 6000 mg. per day. The medication was most effective for conduct disturbances and least effective for the schizophrenic patients. These differences are consistent with hypotheses 8, 9, and possibly 10 and 22. Improvement was described for 65% of the patients. Since no explicit comparison was made between the placebo and the non placebo phases, no compelling argument concerning efficacy was presented in this report. It is interesting to note, however, that the abrupt withdrawal of meprobamate was described as resulting in sharp increases in tension, agitation, and anxiety. Convulsions and tantrum-like seizures were observed in two of the children.

Perlstein (1956) has described the use of meprobamate in convulsive disorders. His sample of 130 patients comprised children, 60 with seizures and 70 with other neurological conditions. The dosages tended to be large and ranged as high as 6400 mg. per day. As a rule the initial dosage was about 600 mg. per day and was increased until benefit or drowsiness occurred. For those patients for whom the medication was effective, changes tended to occur within an hour or two.

The patients who showed a positive response were subsequently given placebo, and a positive evaluation for meprobamate was reported only when the symptoms reappeared with placebo. The data were summarized with respect to degree of efficacy found in various subclasses of patients. The best results were with patients with idiopathic petit mal; 83% were benefited (15 out of 18), and none was made worse. The result with idiopathic seizures of all kinds was quite good compared with the response among patients with an organic brain disease. Although the meprobamate was not found to be as complete or rapid in its full effect as trimethadione, there were no toxic effects accompanying meprobamate. It was concluded that the efficacy of meprobamate may be ascribed to the fact that it diminishes the emotional stress which often contributes to epileptic attacks in predisposed patients, an interpretation which corresponds with hypothesis 12.

The value of meprobamate in the management of cerebral palsy was described in a report by Katz (1958). Although the study was neither blind nor formally controlled, the conditions appear to confer some informational value on the results. Ten of 19 children in a cerebral palsy school were placed on meprobamate medication. The children ranged from 5 to 24 years of age, and their intelligence ranged from the normal level downward. The study was continued for a period of 80 weeks, and the treatment began with a very low dosage level with increments at the end of every two weeks until a satisfactory response was attained. Since the performance of the patients prior to therapy was known, each patient could serve as his own control. It was observed that the 10 children on meprobamate treatment made exceptionally good progress, while the 9 children not participating in the meprobamate trials continued to progress at their original retarded rate. Unfortunately, the way in which the participants and the nonparticipants were selected was not indicated.

In the opinion of the investigator, the appropriate dosage level appeared to vary from patient to patient. The primary therapeutic response was identified in terms of muscle relaxation which usually occurred within three to seven days after the effective dosage level had been reached. Benefit was observed in several respects. It became easier to put on or take off outer clothing, and installing and adjusting braces came to take much less time. Sleep patterns also improved, and there was a general increase in endurance. This increase in endurance was often reflected in greater willingness to perform, and there was an acceleration in reading among the five patients capable of reading. In the investigator's opinion, the drug induced an alleviation of muscle spasms and involuntary movements, contributing to endurance and attention span with consequent improvements in classroom performance. When one considers the probable unpleasant anticipation of muscle spasms and impaired performance by these children, these beneficial results of meprobamate may be viewed as consistent with the provisions of hypotheses 17 and 18, as well as those of hypotheses 12 and 14.

Kraft et al. (1959) described a study of disturbed children ranging in age from 8 to 12 years. The sample was heterogeneous in nature and included behavior disorders, enuretics, schizophrenics, and stutterers. There were 10 control cases drawn from the behavior disorders and the enuretics. There were no control patients drawn from the stutterers or schizophrenic groups. No placebo was administered to the control group. Placebo was given for one month to the treatment group prior to the five month period of meprobamate medication. The usual dosage range was from 200 to 800 mg. daily, but one patient received as much as 1200 mg. All subjects were seen for a total of four visits, an initial evaluation and subsequent evaluations after one, three, and six months. Assessments were in the form of a psychiatric rating, a psychologist's behavior rating, and the Draw-A-Man, the Bender-Gestalt and a Porteus Maze Test. The patients were rated by a psychiatrist on 24 different symptoms. On the average, 30% showed improvement while on placebo, and 53% showed improvement after five months of meprobamate treatment. The specific symptoms where meprobamate showed the greatest relative gain were hyperactivity, nail biting, and reading disability. While on placebo, 33% of the stutterers improved, and after meprobamate treatment an additional 38% had improved. The highest rate of improvement was found in the behavior disorders and substantial improvement was found in the stutterers and enuretics, but apparently no appreciable improvement was found among the schizophrenic children. The improvement found in behavior disorders is anticipated in hypotheses 9 and 22, and the benefit to stutterers, as well as the improvement in reading, is consistent with the provisions of hypotheses 1, 17, and 18. The failure reported for the schizophrenic children appears to be consistent with the implications of hypotheses 8 and 10. It is interesting to note that improvements were reflected in rating scales and general clinical evaluation; important changes were not revealed by the psychological tests.

Alcoholics

In 1957, Greenberg et al. published an evaluation of meprobamate in the treatment of alcoholism. One hundred sixty-seven patients were involved, 100 of whom were hospitalized with acute symptoms of psychomotor agitation, anxiety, irritability, nervousness, and apprehension. Sixty-seven were chronic outpatient alcoholics. Half the patients received drug and half placebo under double blind conditions. The outpatients received 1600 mg. per day and the hospitalized patients received 2400 mg. The duration of treatment was three weeks for the outpatients and from one to two weeks for the hospitalized patients. The patients were assessed on the basis of a check list of pertinent signs and symptoms. Among the outpatients the rate of symptomatic remission under meprobamate was 76% which provides a significant contrast with the 36% for the placebo group. Among the symptoms where the difference in favor of meprobamate was statistically significant were psychomotor agitation, anxiety, irritability, insomnia, depression, and demand for medication. These changes are consistent with the processes of hypotheses 1, 2, 7, 14, 16, and 22. Among the hospitalized patients, the only specific symptom which revealed a significant advantage for meprobamate was insomnia. When rated for general improvement, the superiority for the meprobamate group was statistically significant. It was observed that the duration and the intensity of the hangover, as well as the need for additional medication, were clearly diminished in the meprobamate group, a result consistent with hypothesis 4.

In 1958, Ditman et al. described a crossover study of alcoholic patients where phenaglycodol, phenobarbital, meprobamate, and placebo were assigned in random order for two-week periods. The dosage units were 300 mg. and 30 mg. for phenaglycodol and phenobarbital, respectively, and 400 mg. for meprobamate. Four dosage units were administered each day. The medication program was conducted on a double blind basis. Brief weekly interviews were conducted to evaluate the patients with respect to eight different symptomatic and behavioral criteria. There was a significant difference between the meprobamate and the placebo groups with respect to anxiety and a significant difference between the phenobarbital and placebo groups with respect to sleep. The reduction in anxiety can be consonant with several hypotheses, particularly hypotheses 1 and 2, but the lack of significant improvement in sleep does not meet the provisions of hypothesis 14. Overall evaluations based on the combined criteria led to the conclusion that meprobamate and phenaglycodol were better than placebo for this population. In this outpatient sample, none of the drugs was associated with a lowered incidence of drinking. Side effects were most conspicuous among the patients who were on placebo and phenobarbital.

Martens (1960) reported a double blind comparison of meprobamate and emylcamate. The sample comprised 60 alcoholics. All of the patients were sober at the time of the investigation and were familiar with meprobamate as a prior treatment. Each patient was on each of the treatments for a block of 8 days. In this crossover comparison, the various possible sequences were assigned in counterbalanced fashion. The patients were asked to evaluate each drug by comparing it with their known prior experience with meprobamate. In this evaluation, patients considered both the tranquilizing or relaxing result and the inconvenience of any side effects. Both meprobamate and emylcamate were considered by the patients to be as active or more active than they remembered meprobamate. In most instances, placebo was described as having no effect. Although the exact nature of this effect is not clear, it appears to be consistent with hypothesis 1.

Anxiety and Related States Among Outpatients

One of the early reports concerning the efficacy of meprobamate in the treatment of patients with neurotic symptoms was described by the Danish investigators Hertz and Kronholm (1957) in a double blind placebo controlled investigation. The patients were evaluated with respect to a standard list of symptoms. Severe symptoms were not controlled, but meprobamate was found to be effective for the habitual neurotic symptoms. The dosage was maintained at a moderate level of 1200 mg. per day, and the treatment continued for three weeks. These results are not presented in sufficient detail to relate them to any specific hypotheses.

Since states of anxiety may be found among almost all classes of persons, patient and nonpatient alike, the characteristic of persons in whom anxiety may be allayed by the administration of meprobamate becomes a matter of practical interest. Brick et al. (1958) assigned meprobamate or placebo to 27 prison inmates whose anxiety and tension were considered to be due to confinement. There were 16 prisoners in the meprobamate group and 11 in the placebo group. Four hundred mg. tablets were administered t.i.d. and the treatment continued for an 8 week course. The complaints included anxiety, tension, headaches, loss of appetite, insomnia, irritability, and restlessness. The assessments included the Rorschach, the Taylor Anxiety Scale, and the Bernreuter Inventory. Subjective evaluations for treatment were also noted. From the subjective standpoint, 69% of the patients in the meprobamate group reported improvement as contrasted with 27% for the placebo group. The Taylor Anxiety Scale revealed a higher portion of favorable change in the meprobamate group than in the placebo group, as did the self-confidence and the sociability scales of the Bernreuter. Several aspects of the Rorschach also clearly favored the meprobamate group. Among these were the total number of responses, the number of movement responses, and the number of human movement responses. The authors commented optimistically about the possibility of using meprobamate in prison populations and emphasized that the subsample employed in the present study comprised special confinement cases made up of particularly troublesome individuals who were unable to get along with the administration, fellow inmates, or themselves.

Subsequently in a 1959 study, Brick et al. continued their work with anxious and tense prisoners. Fifty-nine men were divided at random into two groups, a group of 26 receiving placebo and a group of 33 receiving meprobamate in long release form in the amount of two 200 mg. capsules per day. The treatment continued for 8 weeks on a double blind basis. In terms of Rorschach responses, the reduction of neurotic traits in the meprobamate group was much greater than the reduction in the placebo group. Although the present analyses do not describe the response of the patients in terms of direct significance to most clinicians, the data do indicate that meprobamate can effect desirable changes in nonpsychiatric patients who were suffering anxieties and tensions which appear to have a situational origin. These results reported by Brick and his collaborators are consistent with the provisions of hypotheses 1, 9, 22, and perhaps 7 and 14 as well.

In 1958, Hinton reported a study of 40 English outpatients who were suffering from anxiety and tension. Patients who ranged from 18 to 60 years of age were assigned either to meprobamate or placebo on a double blind basis and received 1600 mg. daily throughout the four weeks of treatment. A standard set of 7 symptoms was rated before treatment and at the end of each successive week. Anxiety, phobic-compulsive symptoms, and tension showed significantly greater improvement in the meprobamate group than in the placebo group. These results are consistent with hypotheses 1, 2, and 11. Appetite, somatic pains, depressions, and interestingly enough sleep, did not show a significant advantage for meprobamate. Here it appears that the requirement of hypothesis 14 was not met. Whether hypotheses 4 and 7 should have been applicable is debatable; the issue of secondary gains, hypotheses 3 and 7, was not clarified.

A group of thirty male residents of a Veterans Administration domiciliary was involved in a comparison of phenaglycodol (1200 mg.), meprobamate (1600 mg.), and placebo (Zukin et al., 1959). All the patients were ambulatory and had a diagnosis of primary or secondary anxiety of a chronic nature. The medication was administered on a double blind basis without the patients' knowing that any changes in medication were involved during the six weeks trial. Actually a crossover procedure was employed with each patient receiving a new medication at the end of each two-week period so that every patient received each of the three medications. From the standpoint of an overall rating of improvement, both active medications were superior to placebo, and meprobamate was superior to phenaglycodol. The meprobamate patients showed a significantly greater improvement than the placebo patients with respect to sleep, anxiety, appetite and mood. These results are consistent with hypotheses 2, 4, and 14. The phenoglycodol patients were also significantly superior to the placebo patients in certain respects, specifically sleep, anxiety, and mood. Meprobamate was more effective than phenaglycodol with respect to improvements in sleep, appetite, and anxiety.

Meprobamate was compared with prochlorperazine, sodium amobarbital, and placebo by Rickels et al. (1959) in a double blind crossover study. Each patient was continued on each of the treatments for a two week period under the following daily dosage schedule: meprobamate (1600 mg.), prochlorperazine (20 mg.), and sodium amobarbital (120 mg.). The patients, all selected from a medical outpatient clinic, were described as a heterogeneous group with the diagnosis of psychoneurosis or character neurosis. The primary symptoms were anxiety and tension. Many of the patients had somatic complaints, and mild depression was prevalent. Severe depressions and patients with a definite somatic disorder were excluded. The age ranged from 25 to 60 years. The criteria comprised inventories, checklists, and rating scales.

Although 51 patients began the study, only 28 completed it. Sixteen patients dropped out after the first visit and seven more dropped out after the second or subsequent visits. The visits were scheduled at two-week intervals, and at each visit the patient was given a two-weeks supply of medication. The treatment preceding dropout was not identified, but it was indicated that 10 of the dropouts had received prochlorperazine during the course of treatment, nine had received amobarbital, seven had received placebo, and only two had received meprobamate.

The analysis of the data revealed that when on active medication patients showed more improvement than when on placebo. This was found not only for general estimates of improvement, but also for the ratings for certain symptoms, particularly anxiety, depression, and irritability. The reduction in anxiety and depression are anticipated by hypotheses 2 and 7, but none of the deductions hypothesizes a reduction in unspecified irritability as a response to meprobamate. (Is it possible that the reduction in irritability should be related to a reduction in the somatic complaint of hypotheses 4?) There was also an analysis of the patients to indicate the medication which they found to be most helpful. Meprobamate was first choice for 17 patients, and prochlorperazine was first choice for 7.

A similar study was conducted about the same time by Uhlenhuth and his collaborators (1959). The group of psychiatric outpatients was assigned in counterbalanced manner to two different groups. The group excluded patients with brain syndrome, alcoholism, psychoses, or severe defect of character or intelligence. The medications compared were meprobamate, phenobarbital and placebo. In this crossover design, each patient received every treatment for a two-week period. At the beginning of treatment and every two weeks thereafter, each patient was given a supply of medication and assessed on the basis of a brief interview of from 10 to 20 minutes. The interviews were largely devoted to the patient's assessment and included both an overall judgment and a symptom checklist.

It was found that 42 or 81% of the initial 52 patients were improved. The response to each treatment was analyzed by comparing the patient's posttreatment status with his premedication status. The patients had been assigned to either of two psychiatrists, and for the patients of one psychiatrist, the response to active medication was not found to be different from the response to placebo. For the patients of the other psychiatrist, however, both meprobamate and phenobarbital were more effective than placebo with respect to both the patient's overall estimate of his improvement and the psychiatrist's overall estimate of the patient's improvement. Meprobamate was superior to placebo with respect to the psychiatrist's checklist as well. The psychiatrist whose patients showed no advantageous response to medication had not expected any one agent to be more effective than the other, while the physician whose patients responded advantageously to the medication had been optimistic about the efficacy of the active medication relative to placebo. It may be noted that the treatment was conducted on a double blind basis, and throughout the study neither psychiatrist was able to identify correctly the patients who were on placebo. Unfortunately, this description of the effect of medication is much too general to apply any of the specific hypotheses.

In 1959, Uhr, Pollard, and Miller reported a rather extensive assessment of meprobamate, Tranquil (an over-the-counter preparation of bromides), and placebo. The subjects comprised 32 anxious patients. Most of these were referred by a psychiatrist in private practice; the balance was drawn from a survey of a large number of volunteers or from student health referrals. The patients were treated through three successive 21 day periods of medication. The sequence in which the medication was given was counterbalanced, and most of the conditions for double blind were observed except that the tablets for each medication had a distinctive form. The daily dosage was 1600 mg. meprobamate, or five Tranquil tablets (the recommended maximum), or five placebo tablets. Three kinds of criteria were used. At the end of each medication period all patients received a battery of psychomotor tests, a psychiatric interview, a self-report, and a family report schedule. These schedules for self-report and family report were used at the end of every week throughout the treatment period. The measures taken at the end of the 21 day treatment period were compared for each of the three treatments. The differences between the three treatment groups with respect to the psychomotor tests were small, and only very few of the possible comparisons were statistically significant. Compared with placebo, both of the active medications showed a slight slowing of reaction time. With meprobamate there was a slight improvement in attention. The psychiatrist's estimation indicated that the meprobamate patients appeared to be more rested, more active, but less tense than the placebo patients. There was improvement in their sleeping, but they reported a reduced appetite and an increased requirement of effort in order to conduct day-to-day activities. The reduced tension and improved sleeping are reminiscent of hypotheses 1 and 14. The meprobamate patients slept more and seemed to require more sleep in the daytime, particularly the volunteers who came without referral. Tranquil patients showed a decrease in appetite and a greater requirement for physical effort in the same manner as the meprobamate patients. Any change in attention was negative in the Tranquil group, and the psychiatrist did not rate them as feeling better. Although the patient's self-report revealed no advantage for the treatment groups, ratings by family or close associates revealed changes associated with medication. On this basis there was a significant decrease in anxiety among the meprobamate patients, hypothesis 2. This improvement was apparent for the most anxious patients under Tranquil as well. Thus it is apparent that meprobamate is associated with improvements which are apparent both to the psychiatrist and to associates of the patient.

There are indications that in anxious patients meprobamate may have effects that may not be observable among normal subjects. Such a possibility is drawn to our attention explicitly by a report by Parigi and Biagiotti (1957) who used projective tests in order to examine effects of meprobamate at a dosage level of 1200 mg. to 1600 mg. over a period of 15 days. No appreciable changes were reported for the 10 normal subjects, but for 15 depressive patients greater interest and concentration and improved imagination-ideation were described by the investigators. For example, in both the Rorschach and the TAT performance there were a shorter latency of response, a greater participation in the tests, with the production of more material, and better interpretive content, a result in keeping with hypothesis 7.

There were later studies which continued to indicate the efficacy of meprobamate in the management of neurotic symptoms. For example, in 1963, Bojanovsky and Chloupkova described a study of 22 neurotic women with important anxious-depressive symptoms. In this study, meprobamate was compared with chlordiazepoxide in a double blind, placebo-controlled crossover design. Chlordiazepoxide was administered at 60 mg. per day and meprobamate at 2400 mg. The procedure was one where all patients were placed on placebo for three days, then randomly assigned either to meprobamate or to chlordiazepoxide for one week. After an intervening three-day placebo period, the treatments were switched for an additional week of medication. There was a terminal three days of placebo treatment. Both drugs were described as clinically efficacious with no significant differences between them. Among these patients, anxiety and sleeping disturbances were the most responsive symptoms, see hypotheses 1 and 14.

Dickel et al. (1962) had also reported a comparison with chlordiazepoxide. Their study was based on 36 outpatients with symptoms of anxiety, tension, and depression. In this crossover design, each of three medications (meprobamate, chlordiazepoxide, and phenobarbital) was given in double blind sequence. The dosage units were 400 mg. of meprobamate, 10 mg. of chlordiazepoxide, and 3/4 gr. of phenobarbital. From three to four units comprised the daily medication. The weekly evaluations included the patient's self-description of symptomatic relief, physician's rating, and several objective tests. Eighteen of the patients judged themselves to be improved while on meprobamate; only six had similar reports while on chlordiazepoxide, and two while on phenobarbital. This pattern of response was reflected in the observations of the professional staff. In examining their data, the authors observed that meprobamate was most effective in treating anxiety-tension or anxiety-depression. Anxiety accompanying schizophrenic features or an organic condition was not especially responsive to meprobamate. This pattern of results is consistent with hypotheses 1, 2, 7, and 8.

In 1964, Rickels and Snow reported a study where both meprobamate and phenobarbital were compared with placebo. The investigation comprised two parallel studies and was conducted with anxious, neurotic patients drawn from either psychiatric or medical outpatient clinics. Meprobamate was administered at the rate of 1600 mg. per day and phenobarbital at the rate of 60 mg. per day. The patient's response was evaluated on the basis of successive ratings by the physician and by successive self-descriptions based on formal checklists and inventories. In this double blind crossover study, the medication was changed after two weeks so that the patients who began on medication were taking placebo the last two weeks and *vice versa*. Favorable responses were observed for the meprobamate group, and the writers noted that the greatest change was observed in those who had initially severe symptoms. Such an observation may be based on an artifact, however; maximal gain is possible where the initial severity is most marked, and, of course, the normal regression toward the mean is always greatest for the most extreme cases. There were also fewer dropouts during meprobamate medication, and this difference in dropout rate was considered to be an evidence for the efficacy of meprobamate. It is not possible to specify which particular hypotheses this study could relate to, but a general improvement in anxious patients appears to be consistent with hypothesis 2.

In the Rickels and Snow report (1964), the meprobamate-placebo contrasts were found to be much more favorable than the phenobarbital-placebo contrasts. In the same year (1964), however, Abruzzi reported a study wherein a long release form of pentobarbital was compared with meprobamate. In this report, both medications were considered to be effective. There was a slight, but not statistically significant preponderance of "excellent" results in the pentobarbital group.

Since the kind of alleviation of anxiety which occurs in consequence of meprobamate treatment is similar to the effects which accompany the reassurance of psychotherapy, there continues to be some question about the efficacy of meprobamate among persons who are receiving psychotherapy. Some investigators have been unable to show the beneficial effects of minor tranquilizers in the treatment of anxiety among patients receiving psychotherapy. Rickels and his collaborators (1966) reported a comprehensive study which was directed toward this question. All of the patients in this investigation were receiving psychotherapy in private psychiatric practice. They were assigned on a double blind basis to either meprobamate or placebo and were continued on treatment through a period of six weeks. A set of criterion measures which included symptom rating scales, as well as personality inventories, was applied at the end of the second, fourth, and sixth weeks. Several analytical principles were applied to the data, including analyses of covariance. There were very few dropouts, and of the initial group of 108 (55 on meprobamate and 53 on placebo), ninety-eight finished the sequence. The superior response of the group receiving meprobamate was indicated in several ways, including global estimates and specific symptom ratings. The symptoms showing a significant advantage for meprobamate were obsessive-phobic, sleep disturbance, anxiety, irritability, and depression. These improvements would be consistent with hypotheses 2, 7, 11, and 14. No particular advantage was found for the symptoms of headache, somatization, or hypochondriasis. This result is reminiscent of earlier reports which indicated that hysterics were not benefited by meprobamate (Heller et al., 1957). If the somatic symptoms in Rickels' outpatients were hysterical in origin, the failure to respond to meprobamate is consistent with hypothesis 3. Although the Clyde Mood Scale showed some significant differences, no important trends were revealed by the various IPAT inventory scores (Cattell and Scheier, 1963).

Most studies contribute little insight into either the characteristics of persons most likely to respond favorably to meprobamate or the exact nature of the favorable response. This lack of insight is despite the fact that many of the investigators have used a diverse set of criteria. For example, in 1965, Janecek and others used 18 carefully selected outpatients in a double blind crossover study for the purpose of comparing meprobamate with an experimental compound. All of the patients in this sample were suffering from anxiety and tension; none was psychotic, and none had an organic impairment. They were relatively young patients with a mean age of 35 years. The maximum dosage for meprobamate was 1600 mg. per day, and the study provided two three-week medication periods preceded by and separated by periods of placebo treatment. A psychiatric rating based on an interview and an inventory (MAS) based on the MMPI were used as assessments before and after each period of medication. The symptom ratings showed a definite advantage for the meprobamate treatment from the standpoint of reduction of anxiety and tension. These findings are consistent with hypotheses 1 and 2.

In 1965 also, Uhlenhuth et al. treated a group of 164 anxious adult psychoneurotic patients on an outpatient basis for a period of six weeks. These patients were assigned to either meprobamate or placebo on a double blind basis with dosage at 1600 mg. per day. The patients were evaluated in terms of a mean target symptom score. The meaning of this score varied somewhat from patient to patient because the symptoms on which the patient was assessed after treatment were the ones he had indicated when he filled out the symptom checklist prior to treatment. Meprobamate was more efficacious than placebo whether or not the patient took all the medication prescribed. Unfortunately, the nature of the changes are in no way specified and cannot be related to any of the hypotheses.

Psychiatric Inpatients

In 1957, Heller et al. compared meprobamate with placebo by using a sample of 32 inpatients characterized by the symptoms of tension, particularly restlessness, insomnia, headaches, irritability, and panic. The treatment period of four weeks involved either 1600 mg. of meprobamate daily or an indistinguishable placebo. There were 16 patients in each of the treatment groups. The analysis of the results revealed that 11 patients showed no improvement at all; 8 of these were in the placebo group and three were in the drug group. Among the patients classified as hysterics, there was no appreciable improvement in either the meprobamate or the placebo group. This failure with the hysteric patients is anticipated by hypothesis 3. Nineteen of the patients in the sample were described as dysthymics, nine of whom showed a major improvement; eight of these nine had received meprobamate. When the dysthymic patients were examined from the symptomatic standpoint, the meprobamate group showed significantly greater relief of tension than the placebo group. This advantage for the dysthymic patient appears to be consistent with hypotheses 1 and 7.

In a report from St. Hans Hospital, Denmark, Mogens Hertz (1958) described a double blind study based on a mixed group of inpatients. The sample comprised 41 patients, 21 of whom were considered to be neurotic and 20 psychotic. During the first three weeks, all patients were given meprobamate at daily dosage levels ranging from 1200 mg. to 6600 mg. At that time, some of the patients were continued on meprobamate, while others had been preselected for a switch to placebo. After an additional three weeks of treatment, the medications were exchanged for a final three-week period. The patients were assessed from the standpoint of a standard set of 17 symptoms. It was found that in the neurotic group the response to meprobamate was more favorable than the response to placebo with respect to several symptoms. In the psychotic group, however, the advantage for meprobamate was less marked. The symptoms showing the greatest gain in the neurotic group were tensions and apprehensions. The failure for the psychotic patients is anticipated by hypothesis 8, while the reduction in tension and apprehension is consistent with hypothesis 1. In view of the high dosage levels involved, it is noteworthy that no withdrawal reactions were reported.

The low dosage administration of meprobamate in the control of insomnia among psychiatric inpatients was reported by Hinton and Marley (1959). The patients were male and ranged in age from 22 to 70 years. Of the 11 patients involved, 8 were depressed. The study comprises two series of crossover trials. The first series of 9 nights was divided among three medications: meprobamate at a 400 mg. level, meprobamate at an 800 mg. level, and placebo. A second series of 9 nights was divided among meprobamate at 800 mg., pentobarbital at 200 mg., and placebo. The effect of the drug was assessed in terms of the degree of movement during sleep, the nurse's ratings of soundness of sleep, and the patient's rating of his sleep. From the standpoint of movement of the bed, the data reveal that meprobamate at 800 mg. was significantly superior to placebo in both series. The nurse's rating also revealed that meprobamate was superior to placebo at both the 400 mg.

and the 800 mg. dosage levels. The patient's ratings revealed a similar indication of efficacy. The medication was crushed in fluids and administered orally. The trials were described as double blind. This benefit for insomniacs is anticipated by hypothesis 14.

In 1957, Hollister and his collaborators described the use of meprobamate in chronic hospitalized patients. A total of 191 patients was involved to comprise a series of studies. The first two, based on 37 and 24 patients respectively, involved placebo controls. Global improvement was rated by the psychiatrist. The usual daily dose varied somewhat with the diagnosis and ranged from 800 mg. to 8000 mg. per day with most patients receiving treatment of 3200 mg. or more. Marked improvement was described for anxiety reaction, and the improvement among the schizophrenic reactions was significant among those where anxious and somatic symptoms were prominent and only a mild level of psychosis was apparent. The reduction in anxiety is consistent with hypothesis 2 and the implied reduction of somatic symptoms may be related to hypothesis 4 on the assumption that these somatic reactions are a part of an avoidant pattern of response. Beneficial results were observed also among patients with affective disorders, but it was not clear that patients with organic disorders of the brain or with personality disorders could be expected to improve with meprobamate. The relief among patients with anxiety reaction (obtained in 26 out of 35 cases) was characterized by diminution of such symptoms as inner tension, restlessness, insomnia, irritability, and somatic complaints. Thus the results are consistent with hypotheses 1, 4, 14, and possibly 22 as well.

The possibility of using meprobamate in the treatment of hospitalized schizophrenics was described by Laird et al. (1957). The sample comprised three different subgroups. There were eight females, four of whom received meprobamate and four of whom received placebo. The medication was administered on a double blind basis. There was also a comparable group of eight male patients medicated in a similar manner. The dosage for these patients was 1600 mg. per day. There was also a third group of six patients, all of whom received placebo although the examining physician assumed that they were receiving active medication. In the first group, the four women receiving meprobamate showed varying degrees of improvement and were rated by the nurses as easy to handle and more cooperative. The placebo patients were considered to be unchanged or worse in their general behavior. In the second group of patients, the meprobamate patients were again observed to be improved from the standpoint of the nurse's record. In the third group comprising all placebo patients, only one was described as improved. Other ratings and indices were employed which confirmed the tendency for the meprobamate patients to improve more than the placebo patients. When the specific categories of the rating scale were examined, it was found that the patients receiving meprobamate showed improvement with respect to such symptoms as motoric activity, hostile reactions, mimetic expressions, mood, and feeling. In general, these changes appear not to be covered by the hypotheses generated under the avoidant premise. It is possible, however, that some of the resistance implicit in these responses could be related to hypothesis 22. Patients receiving placebo tended to show a loss with respect to these symptoms. Although the total sample was small and no tests of significance were employed, the procedural schedule was adequate and provided a two-week placebo treatment period, a three-month period in which some patients were on placebo while others were on meprobamate, and a terminal period of one month in which all patients were on placebo. The writers note that, when present, the symptoms of tension, anxiety, and panic are allayed by meprobamate (a result consistent with hypotheses 1, 2, and 18), and they conclude with the observation that meprobamate is effective in making institutional psychotic patients more manageable.

Mitchell et al. (1960) studied a group of 60 newly admitted schizophrenic patients for whom electric shock had been prescribed. Most of these patients had never had shock, and their impression of the treatment was based on reports from other patients. Patients were divided on a random basis into either a placebo or a meprobamate treatment group. The medication was applied on a double blind basis two hours before electroshock therapy (EST). The dosage was 800 mg. At the time of medication and at each succeeding thirty-minute interval, data of a physiologic and behavioral nature were gathered. It was found that meprobamate produced a slight clinically insignificant but statistically significant decrease in blood pressure (less than 5 mm. of Hg.). The reference to a significant drop in blood pressure appears to be consistent with hypothesis 21, however.

Muhlfelder and his collaborators (1959) report the use of meprobamate as an aid in psychotherapy with withdrawn hospitalized schizophrenic patients. In the primary study which involved 20 patients, ten were assigned to placebo and ten to meprobamate. They received from 3200 mg. to 4800 mg. a day for a two-month period. The patients, all female, were in psychotherapy of some unspecified nature. In the meprobamate group, 8 of the 10 were judged to have improved and were noted to be more spontaneous and alert, better able to communicate, and more pleasant in their interaction with others. These results are consistent with hypothesis 22. Only two of the 10 placebo patients showed a comparable improvement. Thus the improvement was characteristic of the meprobamate group and was found to contribute to psychotherapy in the sense that patients on active medication became more desirous of getting well and developed a better transference with the therapist. The authors subsequently treated an additional ten patients with meprobamate, and it was reported that 8 became less anxious and withdrawn and more accessible to the therapist, hypotheses 2 and 22.

There are other reports of the effective use of meprobamate in the treatment of schizophrenic patients. For example, in Pennington's 1957 report, 300 patients were treated with meprobamate, with 84% of the patients showing at least some improvement. These were considered the difficult, relatively treatment-resistant patients, and the average dosage was 3200 mg. per day. Of the various subgroups of patients, those with a paranoid diagnosis were found to respond much better than the hebephrenics and organics. Although improvement in paranoia *per se* is not predicted, improvement in negative, resistant qualities in certain patients is provided by hypotheses 18 and 22. One hundred patients were treated in a double blind crossover sequence, where placebo and meprobamate alternated for four-week periods. Sixty percent of the patients were judged to have improved while on meprobamate, while improvement on placebo depended on whether the placebo preceded meprobamate or followed it.

Improvement was quite rare at the end of the placebo sequence when the placebo preceded meprobamate. When placebo followed meprobamate, however, there was substantial improvement over the pretreatment standing, thus indicating that the beneficial effect of meprobamate treatment tended in some manner to continue for some weeks. This may be a consequence of the fact that patients who had been on meprobamate continued in their attempt to reach a more healthful relationship with their environment, i.e., the continuing benefit reported need not be construed as a perseverating effect of meprobamate *per se*, but as an indication of a healthier, more constructive outlook which developed while on meprobamate medication.

In 1957, Tucker and Wilenski reported a double blind study of schizophrenic veteran patients. Each patient had been ill for at least 18 months, and the period of study extended through 18 weeks, with a two-week postmedication period of observation. The dosage range varied from an initial 1600 mg. per day through a maximum of 4800 mg. Several criteria for evaluation were used, including psychiatric interviews and ratings, conferences and ratings with ward personnel, and an anxiety inventory. The patients in the sample had been selected because they had presented symptoms of anxiety and tension. There were 32 patients in the meprobamate group and 31 in the placebo group. It was found at the end of the medication period that there was a statistically significant difference between the two treatment groups with respect to observable indications of anxiety or tension, a result consistent with hypotheses 1 and 2. This advantage was revealed in both the psychiatrist's ratings and the ratings of the ward personnel. The writers commented upon the placebo effect which other investigators have observed early in the course of placebo treatment. They also noted the distress that has been reported when patients are abruptly withdrawn from high dosage levels of meprobamate. The indications of distress included grand mal seizures in two patients and emphasize the importance of gradual withdrawal.

The possibility of using meprobamate advantageously in combination with chlorpromazine in the treatment of disturbed mental hospital patients was examined by Pollard (1959). These were females who were so disturbed during their hospitalization that there had been no period as great as six weeks without drastic means of control required. These patients had all been chlorpromazine failures in the sense that their behavior had not been altered by dosages over 200 mg. daily continued for more than three months. The experimental group of 12 patients was treated for 7-1/2 months with meprobamate at a high dosage level (4800 mg. for the first 40 days, and 9600 mg. thereafter) concurrently with an average daily dosage of chlorpromazine of 366 mg. The comparable control group of ten patients received chlorpromazine alone at a dosage of 440 mg.

Although the physician treating the patients knew the identity of the medication, the criteria were behavior ratings provided by psychiatric nurses who did not know the nature of the medication received by the patient. After the first 14 days, 8 of the 12 patients on the concurrent treatments were observed to be improved. At this time, only two of the patients receiving chlorpromazine alone were improved. During the ensuing weeks of treatment, there was a tendency for some of the patients in the experimental group to relapse, despite the fact that dosage was increased. At the end of the treatment period, the difference continued to be in favor of the concurrent treatments although the number of cases involved was too small to establish the difference as statistically significant. This use of meprobamate was not specifically anticipated by any of the hypotheses, but in view of the extreme forms of treatment these resistant patients had received it is conceivable that some of their disturbance was avoidant in nature and that hypothesis 9 could be applicable here.

There are later papers which describe the advantageous use of meprobamate in the treatment of psychiatric inpatients. For example, in 1961, Toms compared prochlorperazine (Compazine) with meprobamate in the treatment of mild psychiatric disturbances. The dosages varied with a median of 40 mg. per day of prochlorperazine and 1200 mg. of meprobamate. The primary criterion was the MMPI, but a symptom rating scale was used as well. The patients were all recently admitted male veterans and were able to continue on the medication for at least four weeks. The analysis emphasized pretreatment-posttreatment changes. It is interesting to note that the significant improvements in the meprobamate group were with depression, paranoid ideation and social withdrawal. A reduction in paranoia is not predicted by the hypotheses although reduction in avoidance and resistance may be seen as consistent with hypothesis 22, and the reduction in depression could be consistent with hypothesis 7.

The possbility of using meprobamate in the treatment of severe psychiatric cases is not new. As early as 1956 (Collomb et al.), it was reported that meprobamate was rather advantageous in treating chronic insomnia. Although Collomb et al. commented on the general efficacy of meprobamate in treating psychotic and neurotic patients, they emphasize sleep improvement and reduction in tension, hypotheses 1 and 14. Their sample was a mixed sample of 36 patients, 14 of whom were hospitalized because of the severity of their illness.

There are studies where the effect of meprobamate is inferable from the fact that it was as effective as some other, presumably more powerful, tranquilizer. For example, in 1962, McDonald and Gynther used a sample of 36 male patients, 18 of whom were acute schizophrenics and 18 character disorders. The criteria were somewhat atypical for meprobamate and included heart rate, respiration, and galvanic skin responses. These autonomic nervous system measures were gathered at the time of the patient's response to incomplete sentences which were considered to be relevant to the basis of their difficulty. Half of the sample had been assigned to meprobamate and half to prochlorperazine, but there were no significant differences between the effects of these two treatments on the autonomic measures. Apparently meprobamate was as effective in this report as prochlorperazine for these autonomic symptoms, a result consistent with hypothesis 21.

Kissin et al. (1963) studied a group of 102 male psychotic patients who were recently hospitalized and not yet on any program of medication. Each subject was submitted to five successive experimental trials. Each trial comprised a quantity of a drug (800 mg. in the case of meprobamate), a waiting period of one hour in which the drug was to take effect, and a hand writing performance which was recorded for analysis. All the drugs, including meprobamate, produced a diminution in writing pressure, but there was no such change for the placebo group. This modification was considered to be a significant improvement and a desirable consequence of medication. To the extent that handwriting pressure is an indication of tension, this result is consistent with hypothesis 1.

Dosage Considerations

It may be noted that the dosage level chosen by the various investigators varies appreciably. In most instances the chosen dosage was 1600 mg. per day, but much higher dosages were occasionally used, and lower dosages, particularly 1200 mg., were fairly commonplace. Systematic studies to determine the optimal dosage have not come to the writer's attention, but there are investigations which shed some light on this question. For example, in 1963, Bojanovsky et al. reported a comparison between daily dosages of 2400 mg. and 1320 mg. The patients, mostly female, were psychotherapeutic candidates; virtually all could be described as neurotics. The medication sequence was three days at one dosage level, followed by three days of placebo, which, in turn, was followed by three days of the other dosage schedule. In this crossover design, half the patients began at one dosage level, and half at the other. It was found that for the first three days of medication the patients receiving the larger dosage showed the greater benefit, particularly with respect to anxiety and sleeping disorders. These results are consistent with hypotheses 1 and 14. The condition of the patients was noted to deteriorate during the period of placebo medication, and at the end of treatment, the group that had started on the lower medication was considered to have shown the greater benefit. This probably reflected the disadvantage of having the dosage reduced prematurely in the group that was started on the higher medication.

Although higher dosage levels may be more efficacious from the standpoint of symptom control than the lower dosage level, they may also involve greater daytime somnolence and greater risk of withdrawal symptoms, particularly if the medication is terminated abruptly. These considerations are well illustrated in a report by Haizlip and Ewing (1958). They compared responses to 6400 mg. per day and responses to 3200 mg. per day with placebo responses. A sample of 75 hospitalized patients was randomly divided into the three treatment groups. All the patients had been removed from medication for a period of 30 days, and none had a history of convulsion. After 40 days, placebo was substituted without the knowledge of the patient or the data-gathering staff. It was found that the patients who had been receiving 6400 mg. per day were the most relaxed, while the placebo patients were the least relaxed at the end of treatment (hypothesis 1). The differences were quite significant. It was also found, however, that severe and moderate abstinence reactions were most common among the patients receiving 6400 mg. per day. The reactions among those receiving 3200 mg. per day tended to be mild, and the placebo group was almost free of such reactions. The differences between the treatment groups with respect to abstinence reactions was statistically significant. Thus despite its safety, the use of high dosages of meprobamate can involve definite inconveniences and disadvantages.

Conclusions

In general, the hypotheses correspond with the results of the controlled studies with a consistency which provides little basis for refining the hypotheses. There are, however, certain discrepancies which have emerged repeatedly and suggest areas where predictive caution is most necessary.

Specifically, it was found in the Ditman et al. (1958) study of alcoholics that meprobamate failed to improve sleep significantly more than placebo. Friedman (1957) reported that meprobamate was more effective in reducing tension headaches than in reducing migraine headaches, and Perlstein (1956) had found that patients with petit mal seizures responded better to meprobamate than did patients whose seizures were associated with brain damage. If one were to assume that sleeplessness in Ditman's alcoholic patients was, in part, due to neural damage associated with alcohol abuse, the results of these three investigators would appear to suggest that meprobamate may be less effective in controlling symptoms that are associated with brain damage than in correcting symptoms that are primarily functional in nature, i.e., that are associated with acquired avoidant responses.

Pennington (1957) and Toms (1961) report improvement in paranoid patients treated with meprobamate. These findings are inconsistent with the explicit provision of hypothesis 5. It must be remembered, however, that all forms of suspiciousness and rigidity are not necessarily a consequence of projected hostility. They may, instead, be a denial of fear and basically may be motivated more by dispositions toward flight than fight. In such cases, patients who show behavior which has certain paranoid features may be motivated primarily by avoidant tendencies and may, therefore, according to our fundamental premise be benefited by meprobamate. Nevertheless, the application of this analysis to the present data is *ex post facto*. Opportunity should be sought, therefore, to predict the effect of meprobamate for paranoid patients with the differential prediction of benefit based on careful consideration of whether the symptoms were generated primarily by avoidant motives or by expressive, hostile motives. A comparison of the therapeutic responses of these two classes of paranoid patients could be used to confirm the present conceptualizations.

Since the present hypotheses derive from motivational considerations, there will be numerous symptomatic difficulties where the label alone will be an insufficient basis for anticipating the response to meprobamate. The area of somatic complaints is illustrative. When somatic complaints rest primarily on a valid organic basis or when such complaints are an expression of hostile irritation and dissatisfaction, no positive response to meprobamate is anticipated under our present conceptualization. It is possible, however, that many somatic complaints, despite a seemingly irritable quality, are based on fear and express an avoidant tendency which under the basic premise could be ameliorated by meprobamate.

Chapter VI

STUDIES WITH QUALIFIED
OR NEGATIVE IMPLICATIONS

Observations, whether scientific or incidental, which fail to confirm an hypothesis have an uncertain status for that hypothesis. It is possible that the underlying premises which generate the hypothesis are themselves incorrect. It is possible that the hypothesis has been illogically deduced from the basic premises. It is possible that the observations selected are inappropriate for the hypothesis, or that the observational situation is somehow biased or confounded by irrelevant factors. In addition, the hazard of human error in observing, recording, computing or interpreting is ever present and should never be minimized. Because of the nature of proof and the possibility that a valid positive observation may eventually emerge to invalidate a negative generalization, negative results always have indefinite implication. Actually no proposition either positive or negative can ever be proven in any ultimate sense, and this accounts for the convention in science of disproving or refuting negative propositions or null hypotheses, i.e., if enough positive evidence is available to make the null hypothesis improbable on the basis of some convention or other (usually the .05 level of significance), the positive statement of the hypothesis is considered to be an acceptable working principle which "could be true."

Despite the doubtful status of any one negative report, it is possible that there may be sufficient consistency among several negative reports to suggest a re-statement of hypotheses or a re-formulation of basic premises so that the generation of new hypotheses providing for the negative observations, as well as the positive observations, could increase the precision of our conceptualizations. In the present chapter, the available reports which fail to confirm the expected indications of

74

efficacy for meprobamate will be examined from the standpoint of two purposes: (1) identifying conditions or responses which do not yield in response to meprobamate; (2) assessing the extent to which the failures in meprobamate effect are consistent with the provisions of the 22 hypotheses deduced under the avoidant premise. In this way, the most probable responses to meprobamate may assume sharper definition by the identification of improbable responses.

Many of the reports which fail to confirm the efficacy expected for meprobamate have little informational value from the standpoint of clarifying the status of our hypotheses. Upon close examination, most of these studies are found to be ambiguous with respect to the question of efficacy *per se*. It is of interest to defer consideration of the hypotheses in order to review these ambiguous reports and comment on the features which obscure their relevance to the general question of efficacy.

Factors Which May Detract from the Apparent Efficacy of a Drug

In one comparative investigation (Brill et al., 1964) involving a psychotherapy group, a placebo group, and three other drug groups, the patients were white females under 40 years of age who were not psychotic or severely depressed and who represented the kinds of psychiatric disorders that are commonly treated on an outpatient basis. The meprobamate dosage began at 800 mg. per day and was increased on the basis of the therapist's discretion. No trends were apparent at the end of five weeks, but by the end of 10 weeks there was nonsignificant improvement perceived by the therapist in both the psychotherapy and the meprobamate groups when the placebo group was used as a basis for comparison. The only significant improvements were those reported by the patient himself and by his family. The patients on meprobamate considered themselves to be improved in a number of respects, particularly nervousness, happiness, and ability to handle personal situations so that their overall estimate of improvement was highly significant relative to that of the placebo group. The family reported a tendency toward improvement in the same general respects with the ability to enjoy life maintaining a high level of statistical significance. In addition, the social worker surveying data gathered by other social workers provided ratings which showed significant improvement for various facets of the patient's adjustment, particularly symptomatic adjustment and general interpersonal adjustment. Thus, in this study it appears that the rater himself may be a factor in determining whether positive or negative results are obtained. The residents who served as therapists proved to be least sensitive to improvement which was apparent from the social work records, the patient's self-estimate, and one aspect of the family's report. It is possible that the effects of the primary therapies were obscured somewhat, particularly in the view of the therapists, because all patients were described as receiving "some sort of psychotherapy." Thus to some degree the effect of the experimental treatments may have been confounded with the general therapeutic situation in which all patients were placed.

Rickels and his collaborators (1965) examined data from the standpoint of the effect of events in a patient's life on drug response. They found that negative life events have a detracting effect on the kind of improvement that would be associated with drug treatment, while positive events have their greatest effect in patients receiving placebo. Thus external events tended to counteract and obscure the drug-placebo differences, and the most significant differences between drug and placebo were found in the patients for whom no important external events were reported.

The fact that the patient's response to a drug may reflect many extraneous influences has been the subject of study by Uhlenhuth et al. In their 1966 report, the attitude expressed by the physician administering the medication, the nature of the medication (i.e., meprobamate or placebo), and the clinic population were all considered in a study of anxious psychoneurotics free from apparent schizophrenia or organic impairments. The criteria were concerned mostly with checklists and rating scales pertinent to anxious and depressive states. In the clinic where both the patients and the physicians came from relatively low socioeconomic backgrounds, the effect of meprobamate was clearly enhanced among the patients treated by a physician who was playing a suasive therapeutic role. In the other clinics where presumably there were more middle class patients and physicians, the response to meprobamate was better when the physician was taking a reserved, experimental role. It is possible that middle class patients are more reassured by a cautious, conservative position, while patients from a lower economic level are more reassured by a confident, enthusiastic, supportive physician. Thus, whether a given extraneous factor will have an enhancing or detracting influence on drug effects can depend upon the social attitudes and values of the patients and perhaps of the physicians as well.

Park et al. (1965) examined relationships between improvement ratings provided by physicians and improvement ratings provided by patients. The data were drawn from a double blind placebo-meprobamate comparison. The measures employed were global improvement ratings, a target symptom checklist, and an anxiety checklist. It was found that before medication there were significant differences between physician and patient with respect to target symptoms and anxiety estimations. After the first week of treatment, there were no significant differences between them with respect to any of the measures. It was interesting to observe that patients were somewhat more consistent in their ratings than the physicians were, and it was noted that the physicians tended to detect improvement earlier than the patients. It seems possible, however, that the similarity between physicians' and patients' ratings would vary substantially from setting to setting and that a sensitive assessment of drug effects would require a consideration of both the physicians' and the patients' perceptions.

Fisher et al. (1964) reported that the number of dropouts reflected the physician's attitude. Specifically, among the 66 patients who dropped out, 48% were on meprobamate and 63% were on placebo. Nevertheless, the portion of meprobamate dropouts who were seen by a skeptical, experimentally oriented physician was twice as great as the portion of meprobamate dropouts who were seen by a positive, therapeutically oriented physician. In the placebo group, however, the orientation of the physician appeared to have no effect on dropout rate. Apparently physician attitude and drug effect can interact to diminish dropout rate.

The manner in which the expectations of staff and patients either enhance or detract from the apparent effectiveness of the drug requires systematic exploration. It is possible for a familiar drug to acquire an "authority" which is unwarranted on the basis of its intrinsic effects. It is possible also for a relatively mild drug to become underestimated, particularly if its effect is moderate and not accompanied by conspicuous side effects. In a cleverly simple study involving 40 neurotic inpatients, Bojanovsky and Chloupkova (1966) compared meprobamate in the familiar form with meprobamate in disguised form and discovered that the disguised meprobamate medication was perceived as much more efficacious than meprobamate in its recognized form. The motives and circumstances which make such perceptual biases possible are among the factors which must be controlled or counterbalanced in the study of drug effects and justify the continued use of double blind comparisons.

Koteen (1957) conducted a double blind crossover comparison of meprobamate with placebo. Twenty-five patients were involved in the inquiry, and there were no differences between the two treatments with respect to the number of patients judged to be improved. At least some of the patients were characterized by somatic complaints, mostly neuro-muscular in nature, but the nature of the sample and the conditions of treatment, including duration of treatment, are not described. Accordingly, this negative report provides very few clues. It may be noted, however, that the investigator's attitude toward medication was strictly noncommittal. "At no time was any effort made to persuade the patient that he would be definitely helped by the drug . . . it allowed the patient the privilege of being critical of the medication and *not* of the physician, because he understood that he would be given a more effective capsule on his next visit." In view of the various studies showing the importance of the therapist's attitude in the use of pharmacotherapies, the reserve of this therapist may be suspected as having had a suppressive effect on therapeutic response. There are other reports where the medication was presented to the patient with instructions which would tend to suppress the perceived therapeutic contribution of any medication and to sensitize the patient to other influences. For example, Cytryn et al. (1960) instructed the parents of juvenile patients that the medication would make the children feel better while the satisfying effect of psychotherapy was being established. It is possible that the manner in which the medication was presented contributed to the fact that there were no significant contrasts between the drug groups (meprobamate and prochlorperazine) and the placebo group.

The type of symptomatic amelioration that is sought by the use of minor tranquilizers commonly occurs early in response to psychotherapy. The possibility of psychotherapeutic effects being common to all comparison groups and thereby obscuring any treatment differences had been anticipated in drug testing as early as 1958 by Solomon et al. In their inquiry psychiatrists spent 15 minutes with each patient in order to keep all members of this outpatient sample in treatment. There were significant improvements in all treatment groups, including both a meprobamate and a placebo group, but no significant contrasts among the groups. Since many of the complaints of anxiety, tension, and other related forms of distress are episodic in nature and tend to remit spontaneously, it would seem possible that the longer such patients are held in treatment the less conspicuous is any contrast between a placebo group and a group receiving a minor tranquilizer, such as meprobamate.

In 1958, Coleman et al. used several criteria in a comparison of patients' response to meprobamate and placebo. There were no significant differences in average outcome although some of the MMPI scores approached significance. The ratings by psychiatrists, psychologists, and the patient's self-evaluation were inconclusive. In view of the fact that the average dosage was sufficient (from 1200 to 2400 mg. per day) and the patients were appropriate, the lack of placebo differentiation would have been at least puzzling were it not mentioned in the procedure that the population from which the sample was drawn comprised patients beginning psychotherapy at the mental hygiene clinic. It would appear, therefore, that the inconclusive outcome of what might be generally described as a well conducted study may be ascribed to the fact that psychotherapy could generate in the placebo patients certain changes not unlike those which commonly occur in consequence of the use of minor tranquilizers.

In 1959, Adler studied enuresis in 102 Marine Corps recruits. They were assigned on a double blind basis to meprobamate or placebo. Dosage started at 1600 mg. per day, and the dosage level was increased to 3200 mg. per day if enuresis continued. Forty-three percent of both treatment groups were considered cured. It should be noted, however, that all of the recruits were receiving psychotherapy throughout the course of treatment, a confounding factor which appears to be important on the basis of other published reports. It may be noticed also that uncured recruits were discharged from the service which may represent an important secondary gain in view of the passive disposition which is described for most enuretics. The obscuring effect of secondary gain is anticipated in hypotheses 3 and 6.

The Cytryn et al. (1960) study was based on patients seen at the Children's Psychiatric Service of the Johns Hopkins Hospital. During the course of three months' inquiry in which meprobamate, prochlorperazine, and placebo were compared, therapy was provided for parent and child. The meprobamate dosage ranged from 800 to 1600 mg. per day. The general procedure provided for medication for seven weeks followed by four weeks of withdrawal and a final evaluation at eleven weeks. Progress was assessed from the standpoint of three areas; home as reported by the mother and the social worker, school as reported by the teacher, and clinic as reported by the physician. Regardless of the patient's diagnosis, improvement did not differentiate between the treatment groups. There were differences in sleep disturbances and temper outbursts which favored the medicated groups over the placebo group, but they were not statistically significant. In view of the fact that all three groups were involved in a substantial psychotherapeutic program, the indefinite consequences of these comparisons render the results inappropriate for evaluating the efficacy of medication in the management of such a sample of children.

In 1961, Lorr et al. provided a report of a collaborative study of Veterans Administration outpatient clinics. This investigation was concerned with the hypothesis that psychotherapy plus tranquilizing medication, i.e., meprobamate or chlorpromazine, would be more effective in reducing anxiety and hostility than psychotherapy alone or psychotherapy with a placebo. The treatment lasted for a period of 8 weeks and after the first week the meprobamate patients were on a standard dosage of 1600 mg. per day. In addition to a weekly conference with physician who provided the medication, patients received 50 minutes of psychotherapy each week. Several criteria were employed, including checklists and self-ratings submitted by the patient and a set of standard ratings and observations provided by the therapist. Analysis of covariance was used to evaluate post-treatment standing in a way to control for differences in pretreatment standing. Despite the care with which the criteria were gathered and the sensitivity of this type of analysis, there were no significant findings to document the efficacy of either the chlorpromazine or the meprobamate group relative to the control group. When the treatment groups were combined, it was apparent that there was significant improvement with respect to most of the criteria, and the authors recognized the possibility that the general beneficial results could have been generated by the common treatment, psychotherapy.

There are several studies where the conditions for meprobamate use were clearly exceptional to common practice. For example, it is not surprising to discover that use of an insufficient amount of medication fails to provide evidence of efficacy. In a 1962 report of an outpatient study, Hankoff et al. employed daily dosages of 600 mg. of meprobamate in comparison with placebo and found no indication of therapeutic change. Chlordiazepoxide at 30 mg. and chlorpromazine at 150 mg. per day were found to be more efficacious than placebo in the same inquiry. Thus, it appears that medication with chlordiazepoxide or chlorpromazine in the conventional dosage range produced evidence of efficacy, while meprobamate used at less than one half the conventional dosage was ineffective.

In a study by Batterman et al. (1959), the nighttime sedating effect of various treatments, including meprobamate and placebo, was examined in groups of outpatients. Most of the patients were described as having a musculoskeletal condition referred to as arthritic. Although anxiety, tension, and related symptoms were described for the patients, it is not clear that they were primarily psychiatric patients, and the sample may have been geriatric in nature. In this study, the daytime administration of meprobamate was not considered to have been satisfactory from the standpoint of nighttime hypnotic effect. In view of the relatively short half-life of meprobamate (about 4 hours), it is not surprising that the daytime administration of meprobamate had little nighttime hypnotic effect.

Collard and Kerf (1962) reported a double blind comparison of chlordiazepoxide, meprobamate, and placebo. The sample was somewhat heterogeneous, comprising neurotics, psychopaths, and melancholia patients. Eight of the 33 were ambulatory; twenty-five were in an open psychiatric department. Weekly clinical examinations were conducted, but psychotherapeutic influences were kept at a minimum in order to avoid a confounding effect. Overall improvement was rated from "none" to "spectacular." In addition, there was similar rating for improvement in certain symptoms, particularly anxiety and irritability-aggressiveness. In this crossover study, the number of patients who were free from anxiety while on medication was not significantly greater than the number who were free while on placebo. It may be noted that treatment with any one substance was continued for one week only and that dosage for meprobamate was low (600 mg. per day for the ambulatory patients and 1200 mg. for the hospitalized patients).

Sometimes improbable characteristics of the sample place the implications of the results in question. For example, in the later collaborative study based on data from different Veterans Administration outpatients clinics, McNair et al. (1965) reported a comparison of chlordiazepoxide and meprobamate with placebo. The treatment continued for eight weeks, and although a standard dosage was prescribed, it is not reported how much medication was actually used by these outpatients. It was stated that patients were dropped from the study if they had not taken at least one capsule on the days of evaluation. Difficulties were encountered in the meprobamate-placebo comparison. The meprobamate group was significantly more disturbed than the placebo group prior to treatment, and the analysis of covariance could not be properly applied to correct for these pretreatment differences because of significant differences between the two groups with respect to pretreatment-posttreatment regressions.

Pertinent Negative Results

Among the studies which fail to provide the usual indications of meprobamate efficacy, several with a negative or qualifying report cannot reasonably be explained in terms of methodological or procedural considerations. These studies are of considerable interest from the standpoint of the various hypotheses deduced under the acquired avoidance premise.

To illustrate, hypotheses 9 and 22 are relevant to aggressive, obstreperous or a least resistant behavior when such behavior serves as an expression of an avoidant motive. Hypothesis 20 anticipates the possibility that meprobamate could lead to acting out behavior among patients whose impulsive expressions have been deterred by the anticipation of punishment. The literature provides three reports of mentally defective patients wherein restless, aggressive, disturbed qualities of behavior did not yield satisfactorily in response to meprobamate medication. It is possible that in these patients the aggressive behavior had no relevance to avoidance motives and was either hostile acting out in consequence of frustration or the kind of irritability that is often associated with brain damage.

In 1958, Heaton-Ward and Jancar studied a sample of 16 female mental defectives with histories of aggressiveness and destructiveness. None was considered to be psychotic. The patients were divided into two treatment groups, and although the meprobamate medication was distinguishable from the control, the fact that meprobamate was involved was not known to the nursing staff. After four weeks, dosage was increased to five tablets or 2000 mg. per day. Despite the use of a standard progress report which was completed at weekly intervals, there was no indication of therapeutic gain. Whether hypothesis 9 should be applicable here cannot be assumed from the report. If the aggression were due primarily to avoidant efforts, evidence of meprobamate effect should have been noted. It is possible that the aggression was an expression of an irritability resulting from neurological damage. It is possible also that the aggression was an expression of the frustration which is so often the lot of mental defectives.

In 1959, Drake reported negative results in the use of meprobamate with 73 mentally retarded female patients with cerebral palsy. Although no control was employed in this inquiry, none was needed since there were no indications of therapeutic benefit. Treatment continued for a period of four months, and for some patients daily doses exceeded 40 mg. per kilogram of body weight. There were some side effects but no withdrawal reactions. These negative reports are congruent with other reports (see positive result section) which indicated that certain defectives were unresponsive to meprobamate.

Rudy et al. (1958) compared several drugs, including meprobamate, from the standpoint of managing a group of active, aggressive, mentally defective patients. Although this group responded to phenothiazine tranquilizers, there was no appreciable response to meprobamate at 400 mg. t.i.d.

The results of these three studies, in combination with some of the comments included in the positive results section, suggest that hypotheses 9 and 22 may not be applicable to aggressively acting out, mentally defective patients. It should be noted that meprobamate was hypothesized not to be effective in the control of the expression of aggression *per se* (see hypotheses 5 and 8).

According to Zucker et al. (1958), meprobamate was not effective in handling the reaction of opiate patients to withdrawal. The sample was divided into three groups, one receiving no supplemental medication, one on an inert placebo, and a third receiving 1200 mg. meprobamate daily. At the beginning of withdrawal, all three groups had been stabilized on methadone. There were no indications that the meprobamate group was benefited, and it was stated that these patients had significantly more muscle tension than the control group receiving no supplemental medication. In view of the beneficial response of withdrawn addicts described in the previous chapter (Gruhzit and Lee, 1959), the negative results in the Zucker study are inconsistent. It is possible that these differences could be reconciled if more details were available. One of the factors that would have to be examined closely is the influence of stabilization on methadone in the Zucker study and whether the apparent lack of meprobamate effect could have been due to the confounding effect of the common methadone experience.

There were other reports which did not relate to the provisions of any of the hypotheses. An illustration is provided by Smith et al. (1957). These investigators compared meprobamate with placebo in the treatment of alcoholic patients who were abstinent following a recent alcoholic bout. Although the meprobamate patients were described as responding no better than placebo patients, the details of the treatment and other relevant aspects are not described in a manner which permits comparison of these results with other studies of alcoholics.

Another situation unrelated to the hypotheses and in which meprobamate has been found to be ineffectual is in the management of tetanus. Damany and Kamat (1958) described an investigation of 66 cases of tetanus admitted to the general hospital at Ahmedabad. In one group of 27 cases, the standard treatment program was followed, and in a second group of 39 cases the standard treatment was supplemented with 6 daily doses of 800 mg. meprobamate each. It was found that the addition of meprobamate did not reduce the mortality rate significantly, nor did it shorten the hospitalization period for the survivors. Although the assignment was not random, it was intended to be unbiased, and the data revealed no evidence of bias. The failure here appears to be unrelated to any of the hypotheses, and these results, combined with the results of the cerebral palsy patients, suggest that meprobamate may be ineffectual when a neuropathy lies at the base of the behavioral disturbance.

In 1960, Carter and Hunter described the use of meprobamate in the management of fearful dental patients. A total of 196 patients was assigned to four different treatment groups, including meprobamate and placebo groups, on a double blind basis. The premedication period was 24 hours, and the meprobamate patients were provided four capsules of 400 mg. each. Two types of criteria were employed: the patient's subjective experiences and the patient's behavior in the dental situation. These criteria were gathered by the dentist on two occasions: when the patient received the premedication and twenty-four hours later at the time of the dental appointment. Regardless of the criteria employed, meprobamate was not found to be superior to placebo as a premedication for dental patients. This finding appears to be exceptional to the provisions of hypothesis 15 and possibly hypothesis 18. A confident interpretation of these results would depend upon a thorough understanding of the patients and the conditions under which they were medicated and assessed. Although the possibility of secondary gain cannot be ruled out, it appears that meprobamate was ineffectual in reducing the avoidant response. In view of the short half-life of the drug, some questions can be raised concerning the relationship between time of ingestion and the time of assessment. There is also the question of how many of these persons were actually in pain at the time of assessment. Meprobamate is not an analgesic and is not considered to be effective in reducing *primary* avoidant responses. The premise relates to the reduction of acquired avoidant responses and relevant motivational dispositions.

The effect of meprobamate has been examined in other situations where the pertinence of the hypotheses to the specific application leaves some room for debate. For example, tranquilizing drugs, including meprobamate, were evaluated by Eslami and Atwell (1958) in the treatment for restless, apprehensive, and uncooperative hospitalized tuberculous patients. In the crossover design, each treatment, including meprobamate and placebo, was given for a two-week interval. The patients were observed daily with respect to 10 major criteria, and no differences were found between meprobamate and placebo treatments. The details of the assignment of the drugs and the sequence in which they were administered were not included. The sample comprised 15 patients. The meaning of the restlessness among the tuberculous patients is not clear. Without specific information to the contrary, it would appear that these results are inconsistent with hypotheses 1, 17, and 22.

In 1957, Folkson reported a crossover study based on psychiatric outpatients, many of whom he considered to be treatment-resistant. The average duration of treatment was two months, and the daily dosage of meprobamate was 1200 mg. to 1600 mg. or more. The fact that only seven of the sample of 41 patients were judged to be improved attests to the treatment-resistant nature of the group. Such a low improvement rate in anxious outpatients is somewhat surprising in view of the usual episodic nature of anxiety. Perhaps in this treatment-resistant sample, there were patients who enjoyed secondary benefit from their symptoms. It will be remembered that such a possibility was suggested in the discussion of the study of enuresis among Marine recruits. It should be noted, however, that improvement can mean many different things. Specifically, it is possible that the target symptom itself may be in remission, but complaints of side effects may be sufficiently conspicuous to lead the therapist to judge the patient as unimproved. It is possible that such a factor was involved in the Folkson study. Seven cases of side reactions were described in his report, including two troublesome instances of skin disturbance.

Conclusions

This review of reports of controlled studies which failed to affirm a therapeutic efficacy for meprobamate has generated relatively little insight. Many of the studies are difficult to associate with an hypothesis because they have been designed in a manner which makes the results *per se* inconclusive or, at least, ambiguous with respect to the efficacy of meprobamate in the situation described. Other studies describe more or less exploratory applications involving situations not implied by the usual applications of the drug or anticipated by the present hypotheses. Almost none of the studies provides a direct and unambiguous contradiction for any one of the hypotheses.

The study of uncooperative tuberculous patients by Eslami and Atwell (1958) showed no ameliorating effect of meprobamate medication despite the fact that the patients were described as apprehensive. This appears to be contrary to the provisions of the present hypotheses, and the report provided no clues which could be used to reconcile the discrepancy. There was a second report which presented unaccountable results. Specifically, Folkson found meprobamate ineffectual in treating outpatients who were described as suffering from severe and treatment-resistant anxiety. In these patients, as in the Eslami and Atwell patients, the possibility of important secondary gains cannot be disregarded.

It is apparent that patients whose disruptive behavior has organic or toxic basis may not respond to meprobamate. This is particularly apparent in studies of mental defectives (Heaton-Ward and Jancar, 1958; Drake, 1959; and Rudy et al., 1958). The tetanus patients of Damany and Kamat (1958) and perhaps the opiate patients of Zucker (1958) belong also in the catagory of treatment failures which may be in part ascribable to neurological factors.

The failure of Carter and Hunter's dental patients (1960) to respond satisfactorily to meprobamate is unexpected in view of several hypotheses, but the possibility that these patients may have been in pain reminds us of the distinction between the distress of an unpleasant anticipation with its avoidant reaction and the distressed avoidant reaction to primary physical pain *per se*.

In addition to the questionable effect of meprobamate in controlling expressive adient behavior, it seems that the use of meprobamate to reduce abient or avoidant behavior may be particularly uncertain when the anxiety and related reactions occur in the presence of brain damage, physical pain, or substantial secondary gains.

Chapter VII

CONCLUSION

The research reports that were available for the present survey appear to be distinctly favorable to the assumption that meprobamate tends to weaken acquired avoidant responses. It must be emphasized, however, that this assumption is only a working premise. Although the hypotheses generated from this premise were supported and only rarely challenged by the published reports, they are only hypotheses and are not conclusions despite their obvious potential for clinical prediction.

The value of hypotheses is not found in their origins, but is established on the basis of their predictive pertinence. The only truly bad hypotheses are those that cannot be tested. Fortunately, the present hypotheses have a rather explicit pertinence to many common situations of clinical interest and should lend themselves to empirical verification or refutation. There are several approaches which may be used to examine the value of the premise that meprobamate reduces acquired avoidant responses. Perhaps the most immediately practical approach would involve the experimental use of situations that reflect the provisions of each of the 22 hypotheses stated in Chapter IV. Each of these hypotheses suggests several experimental approaches, and any list of relevant experimental tests could be only illustrative and not exhaustive.

The 22 hypotheses stated in Chapter IV may not necessarily be the most interesting or the most appropriate hypotheses for testing the practical clinical validity of the major premise. There are many everyday difficulties which seem to be quite pertinent to the meaning of the premise that meprobamate reduces or weakens acquired avoidant responses. The most obvious situations are only quasi-clinical in nature and appear more often in the files of the student advisor than in the records of the clinical psychiatrist.

To illustrate, there are many children who appear to be crippled by shyness to such a degree that their academic work is impaired and their social interactions are a torture. In those cases where the shyness is based on a fear of failure and rebuff, the present conceptualization would lead to the prediction that meprobamate would be helpful. If this shyness were merely an expression of covert resentment or a negativistic attempt to control others, no particular benefit from meprobamate would be predicted. Perhaps stagefright and incapacitating fear and inhibition in an interview situation should also be viewed as acquired avoidant reactions which could be ameliorated by meprobamate. Certainly complaints about this type of discomfort are sufficiently common to provide adequate experimental material, and tests of the efficacy of meprobamate in these situations could be readily designed.

More relevant to the interest of clinicians are the not infrequent cases of crippling sexual inhibitions in the female and impotence in the male. Although these responses are reminiscent of some of the hypotheses stated in Chapter IV, they are distinctive enough to merit separate analysis, and no reports of the controlled use of meprobamate in these situations have come to the writer's attention. In formulating hypotheses pertinent to these problems, care must be taken to recognize diversity in their possible motivational bases. Sexual incapacity, like social incapacity, can be primarily an avoidant response based on the anticipation of unpleasant consequences. Not infrequently, however, it is recognized that such incapacity has hostile origins and represents a disposition to deny, frustrate, or control one's partner or persons symbolized by the partner.

Recurrent in all of these hypothesized applications are assumptions concerning the avoidant significance of the behavior in question. Thus the pertinence of the hypothesis to a particular situation rests on the assumption that the avoidant disposition is a significant part of the difficulty, and the precise clinical application of these hypotheses rests on the ability of the clinician to recognize the nature of the predominant motive contributing to the difficulty. On the basis of the present consideration, the effective use of meprobamate would rest upon correct recognition of the motivational significance of the patient's difficulty. For those problems which could be in the service of either an abient or an adient motive, inability to identify the essential motivating disposition could lead to equivocal therapeutic results. In clinical research, as well as in clinical practice, however, the assessment of pertinent motives is always a desirable if not an essential condition for sound procedures.

In addition to the obvious and immediately practical approach to verification, which could be provided by suitably designed clinical applications, experimental approaches based on fundamental considerations could be rewarding. For example, the research literature contains repeated indications that there are areas of the brain which have a nociceptive significance. When such an area of the brain is stimulated, the ensuing behavior may be described as having an avoidant quality. In some instances, abient or avoidant-type behavior is directly generated by pain and is avoidant only in the sense that it has an escape function. In other instances, the abient response is avoidant in the particular and unique sense that it emerges in anticipation of a noxious situation and may serve to prevent a painful stimulation.

Although meprobamate is not an analgesic and would not be expected to reduce all responses to nociceptive stimulation, perhaps it could be shown that meprobamate tends to reduce the avoidant response to stimulation of some specific portion of the brain which ordinarily generates avoidant behavior. If this were possible, a significant beginning would have been made in delineating the portion of the brain which is involved in the mediation of meprobamate's effect as an agent which reduces acquired avoidant responses. Unfortunately, any attempts of this kind which failed to show a diminution of abient response in consequence of meprobamate medication would have no informational pertinence to the present hypothesis other than indicating that the specific area stimulated had no particular relevance to meprobamate effects. Thus such tests are not critical, and although success could be most instructive, failure in any given brain area would contribute little to the status of the general premise. Nevertheless, if it could be shown that meprobamate reduces the avoidant quality of the behavior which accompanies the stimulation of some particular area of the brain, one could be interested in the possibility that at least part of the effect of meprobamate was localized in that area.

Whatever the action of meprobamate might be on such a brain center, the studies examined in the present survey indicate that the action would be relatively prompt with full effect within an hour, and relatively short-lived with appreciable diminution at the end of four hours. The effect might not be found in the internal bodies of the nerve cell and perhaps not in the cell membrane itself. There could be a vasodilatation or a vasoconstriction of the area in question, or a localized edema. Perhaps there could be some change in the synaptic media, possibly indirectly in the form of some localized suppression or enhancement of enzymatic substances or more directly through localized adrenergic or cholinergic effect.

Summary

The reports of controlled studies of meprobamate comprise a substantial and varied literature. Contrary to expectation, the total literature was not found to elaborate on the functions of meprobamate as a central relaxant and suggests that the anticonvulsant effects may be most apparent in petit mal disorders as contrasted with organic brain disorders or grand mal seizures. Although the literature did not follow the course initially anticipated, it was found to imply a central and persisting theme which could indicate that meprobamate tends to weaken acquired avoidant responses. When employed as a working premise, this inference can be used to generate many hypotheses which are quite pertinent to the clinical application of meprobamate and which have a usefully specific predictive function. Thus the inferred premise and the deduced hypotheses are consistent with most of the available literature. In addition, they suggest specific experimental tests of substantial clinical pertinence and point to a way of conceptualizing the use of meprobamate in treating the individual.

REFERENCES

Abruzzi, W. A.: A long release dose form of pentobarbital compared with meprobamate in the management of anxiety states. *Clin. Med., 71*:1231–1234, 1964.

Adler, H. M.: Enuresis in recruits. *Armed Forces Med. J. 10*:767–786, 1959.

Batterman, R. C., Grossman, A. J., Leifer, P., and Mouratoff, G. J.: Clinical re-evaluation of daytime sedatives. *Postgrad. Med., 26*:502–509, 1959.

Berger, F. M.: The chemistry and mode of action of tranquilizing drugs. *Ann. N.Y. Acad. Sci., 67*:685–698, 1957.

Berger, F. M.: Classification of psychoactive drugs according to their chemical structures and sites of action. In: L. Uhr and J. G. Miller (Eds.) *Drugs and Behavior,* New York, Wiley, 1960.

Blance, P. P., and Gunn-Sechehaye, A.: A new treatment for the vomiting of pregnancy, "Miltown." *Praxis, 47*:758–760, 1958.

Bojanovsky, J., and Chloupkova, K.: Comparison between the effect of Librium and meprobamate on neurosis. *Activ. Nerv. Sup., 5*:220–221, 1963.

Bojanovsky, J., and Chloupkova, K.: A comparison of the therapeutic effect of meprobamate administered in its current appearance and as an unknown drug. *Activ. Nerv. Sup., 8*:440–441, 1966.

Bojanovsky, J., Chloupkova, K., and Horanska, D.: Comparison between medium and large doses of meprobamate in short-time administration. *Activ. Nerv. Sup., 5*:225, 1963.

Boyd, L. J., Cammer, L., Mulinos, M. G., Huppert, V. F., and Hammer, H.: Meprobamate addiction. *J.A.M.A., 168*:1839–1843, 1958.

Boyd, L. J., Huppert, V. F., Mulinos, M. G., and Hammer, H.: Meprobamate in treatment of hypertension. Its effects alone and in combination with mecamylamine. *Amer. J. Cardiol., 3*:229–235, 1959.

Brick, H., Doub, W. H., Jr., and Perdue, W. C.: The effect of tranquilizers on anxiety reactions in penitentiary inmates. *J. Soc. Therapy,
4*:48–54, 1958.

Brick, H., Doub, W. H., Jr., and Perdue, W. C.: A further study on the
effect of meprobamate on anxiety reactions in penitentiary inmates.
J. Soc. Therapy, 5:190–198, 1959.

Brill, N. Q., Koegler, R. R., Epstein, L. J., and Forgy, E. W.: Controlled study of psychiatric outpatient treatment. *Arch. Gen. Psychiat.,
10*:581–595, 1964.

Brittain, R. T.: The pharmacology of 2-amino-4-methyl-6-phenyl-
amino-1,3,5-triazine, a centrally acting muscle relaxant. *J. Pharm.
Pharmac., 18*:294–304, 1965.

Burnstein, E., and Dorfman, D.: Some effects of meprobamate on human
learning. *J. of Psychol., 47*:81–86, 1959.

Caldwell, M. B., and Spille, D. F.: Effect on rat progeny of daily administration of meprobamate during pregnancy and lactation. *Nature,
202*:832–833, 1964.

Carter, W. J., and Hunter, D.: The effects of the psychotherapeutic
drugs, glutethimide, meprobamate and ectylurea on dental patients.
J. Amer. Dent. Hyg. Assoc., 61:444–449, 1960.

Cattell, R. B., and Scheier, I. H.: The IPAT Anxiety Scale Question-
naire. Champaign, Ill., *IPAT,* 1957, 1963.

Chen, G., Bohner, B., and Bratton, A. C., Jr.: The influence of certain
central depressants on fighting behavior of mice. *Arch. Int. Pharmacodyn., 142*:30, 1963.

Cole, H. F., and Wolf, H. H.: The effects of some psychotropic drugs on
conditioned avoidance and aggressive behaviors. *Psychopharmacologia, 8*:389–396, 1966.

Coleman, E. L., Nelson, S. E., Olson, F. P., Raths, O. N., Jr., and
Wiener, D. N.: A controlled study of the use of meprobamate in a
mental hygiene clinic. *J. Clin. Exper. Psychopath. & Quart. Rev.
Psyhiat. & Neurol., 19*:323–329, 1958.

Collard, J., and Kerf, J.: Comparative double-blind study of chlordiazepoxide, meprobamate and a placebo. *Ann. Med-Psych., 1*:921–934,
1962.

Collomb, H., Miletto, G., and Chaupin, M.: Meprobamate in the treatment of psychoses and neuroses. *Rev. du Praticien., 6*:1200–1202, 1956.

Cook, L., and Weidley, E.: Effects of a series of psychopharmacological agents on isolation induced attack behavior in mice. *Fed. Proc., 19*:A22, 1960.

Cytryn, L., Gilbert, A., and Eisenberg, L.: The effectiveness of tranquilizing drugs plus supportive psychotherapy in treating behavior disorders of children: A double-blind study of eighty outpatients. *Amer. J. Orthopsychiat., 33*:113–129, 1960.

Damany, S. J., and Kamat, G. R.: Meprobamate in tetanus. *J. Indian Med. Assoc., 31*:394–397, 1958.

DaVanzo, J. P., Daugherty, M., Ruckart, R., and Kang, L.: Pharmacological and biochemical studies in isolation-induced fighting mice. *Psychopharmacologia, 9*:210–219, 1966.

Davis, W. M.: Neurophysiological basis and pharmacological modification of inhibitory emotional behavior in the rabbit. *Arch. Int. Pharmacodyn., 142*:349–360, 1963.

Di Carlo, L. M., Katz, J., and Batkin, S.: An exploratory investigation of the effect of meprobamate on stuttering behavior. *J. Nerv. Ment. Dis., 128*:558–561, 1959.

Dickel, H. A., Dixon, H. H., Shanklin, J. G., and Dixon, H. H., Jr.: A clinical double-blind comparison of Librium, meprobamate and phenobarbital. *Psychosomatics, 3*:129–133, 1962.

Di Mascio, A.: Drug effects on competitive-paired associate learning: Relationship to and implications for the Taylor manifest anxiety scale. *J. Psychol., 56*:89–97, 1963.

Ditman, K. S., Cohen, S., and Whittlesey, J. R. B.: A clinical comparison of meprobamate, phenaglycodol, phenobarbital and placebo. *Clin. Therap. Rep.,* 541–542, 1958.

Drake, M. E.: Meprobamate in mentally retarded cerebral palsy. *J. Med. Soc. N.J., 56*:256–257, 1959.

Eger, E. I., and Keasling, H. H.: Comparison of meprobamate, pentobarbital, and placebo as preanesthetic medication for reginal procedures. *Anesthesiology, 20,* 1959.

Eisenberg, B. C.: Role of tranquilizing drugs in allergy. *J.A.M.A., 163*:934–937, 1957.

Eslami, V., and Atwell, R. J.: Effect of tranquilizing drugs on hospitalized tuberculous patients. *Am. Rev. Tuberc., 78*:127–130, 1958.

Exton-Smith, A. N., Hodkinson, H. M., and Cromie, B. W.: Controlled comparison of four sedative drugs in elderly patients. *Brit. Med. J., S364*:1037–1040, 1963.

Feldman, R. S., and Lewis, E.: Response differences of psychotropic drugs in rats during chronic anxiety states. *J. Neuropsychiat., 3*:S27–S41, 1962.

Fisher, S., Cole, J. O., Rickels, K., and Uhlenhuth, E. H.: Drug-set interaction: the effect of expectations on drug response in out-patients. *Neuropsychopharmacology, 3*:149–156, 1964.

Folkson, A.: Use of meprobamate in tension states. *J. Ment. Sci., 103*:860–863, 1957.

Frankenhaeuser, M., and Kareby, S.: Effect of meprobamate on catecholamine excretion during mental stress. *Percept. Motor Skills, 15*:571–577, 1962.

Friedman, A. P.: The treatment of chronic headache with meprobamate. *Ann. N.Y. Acad. Sci., 67*:822–826, 1957.

Gantt, W. H.: Experimental studies in animals of the effects of drugs on cardiac stress symptoms. *J. Neuropsychiat., 5*:472–474, 1964.

Greenberg, L. A., Lester, D., Dora, A., Greenhouse, R., and Rosenfeld, J.: An evaluation of meprobamate in the treatment of alcoholism. *Ann. N.Y. Acad. Sci., 67*:816–819, 1957.

Gruhzit, C. C., and Lee, C. O.: The use of meprobamate in the treatment of heroin withdrawal symptoms. *Bull. Narcotic, 11*:6–14, 1959.

Haizlip, T. M., and Ewing, J. A.: Meprobamate habituation. *New England J. Med., 258*:1181–1186, 1958.

Hankoff, L. D., Rudorfer, L., and Paley, H. M.: A reference study of ataraxics. A two-week double blind outpatient evaluation. *J. New Drugs. 2*:173–175, 1962.

Heaton-Ward, W. A., and Jancar, M. B.: A controlled clinical trial of meprobamate in the management of difficult and destructive female mental defectives. *J. Ment. Sci., 104*:454–456, 1958.

Heise, G. A., and Boff, E.: Taming action of chlordiazepoxide. *Fed. Proc., 20*:393, 1961.

Heller, G. C., Walton, D., and Black, D. A.: Meprobamate in the treatment of tension states. *J. Ment. Sci., 103*:581–588, 1957.

Herbring, B. G., and Wiklund, P. E.: Nuncital, meprobamate and placebo in a double blind premedication study. *Acta. Anaesth. Scandinav., 4*:1–4, 1960.

Hertz, M.: Action of Restenil (meprobamate)—a "double-blind" clinical study in a mixed psychiatric ward. *Ugeskr. Laeg., 120*:335–341, 1958.

Hertz, M., and Kronholm, V.: The effect of meprobamate in patients with neurotic symptoms. A clinical double-blind study. *Nordisk Med., 58*:1617–1621, 1957.

Hess, E. H.: Effects of drugs on imprinting behavior. In: L. Uhr and J. G. Miller (Eds.) *Drugs and Behavior,* New York, Wiley, 1960.

Hinton, J. M.: A controlled trial of meprobamate in anxious out-patients. *J. Neurol. Neurosurg. Psychiat., 21*:301–304, 1958.

Hinton, J. M., and Marley, E.: The effects of meprobamate and pentobarbitone sodium on sleep and motility during sleep: A controlled trial with psychiatric patients. *J. Neurol. Neurosurg. Psychiat., 22*:137–140, 1959.

Hoffeld, D. R., and Webster, R. L.: Effect of injection of tranquilizing drugs during pregnancy on offspring. *Nature, 205*:1070–1072, 1965.

Hollister, L. E., Ilkings, H., Hiler, E. G., and St. Pierre, R.: Meprobamate in chronic psychiatric patients. *Ann. N.Y. Acad. Sci., 67*:789–798, 1957.

Holliday, A. R.: Effect of meprobamate on stuttering. *Northwest Med., 58*:837–841, 1959.

Holliday, A. R., Duffy, M. L., and Dille, J. M.: The effects of certain tranquilizers on a stress producing behavioral task. *J. Pharmacol. Exper. Therap. 122*:32A, 1958.

Hughes, F. W., and Kopmann, E.: Influence of pentobarbital, hydroxyzine, chlorpromazine, reserpine, and meprobamate on choice-discrimination behavior in the rat. *Arch. Int. Pharmacodyn., 126*:158–170, 1960.

Jacob, J., and Michaud, G.: The effects of various pharmacological agents (amphetamine, cocaine, caffeine, hexobarbital, meprobamate, morphine, dextromoranide, *l*-methadone, pethidine and 3570 ct) on the exhaustion time and behavior of mice swimming at 20° C. *Med. Exp., 2*:323–328, 1960.

Jacob, J., and Michaud, G.: Effects of different pharmacological agents on the time of exhaustion and the behavior of mice swimming at 20° C *Arch. Int. Pharmacodyn., 133(1–2)*:101–115, 1961.

Janecek, J., Schiele, B. C., Bellville, T. P., Vestre, N. D., and Raths, O.: A controlled study of 4-(1-phenyl-4-piperazinyl)-butyl-3, 4,5-trimethoxybenzate hydrochloride (MA 568) and meprobamate in psychiatric outpatients. *J. New Drugs, 5*:51–56, 1965.

Janssen, P. A. J., Jageneau, A. H., and Niemegeers, C. J. E.: Effects of various drugs on isolation-induced fighting behavior of male mice. *J. Pharm. Exp. Therap., 129*:471–475, 1960.

Janssen, P. A. J., Niemegeers, C. J. E., and Dony, J. G. H.: The inhibitory effect of Fentanyl and other morphine-like analgesics on the warm water induced tail withdrawal reflex in rats. *Arzneim. Forsch., 13*:502–507, 1963.

Jensen, E., Kristjansen, P., and Paerregaard, G.: The effect of meprobamate in neurotic and senile patients. *Nordisk. Med., 58*:1614–1617, 1957.

Katz, B. E.: Education of cerebral palsied children. The role of meprobamate: a preliminary evaluation. *J. Pediat., 53*:467–475, 1958.

Kelleher, R. T., Fry, W., Deegan, J., and Cook, L.: Effects of meprobamate on operant behavior in rats. *J. Pharmacol. Exp. Therap., 133*:275–280, 1961.

Kissin, B., Tripp, C. A., Fluckiger, F. A., and Weinberg, G. H.: Effect of ataractic drugs on motor control in acute hospitalized psychiatric patients. *J. Neuropsychiat., 4*:409–412, 1963.

Kletzkin, M., Wojciechowski, H., and Margolin, S.: Postnatal behavioural effects of meprobamate injected into the gravid rat. *Nature, 204*:1206, 1964.

Koteen, H.: Use of a "double-blind" study investigating the clinical merits of a new tranquilizing agent. *Ann. Int. Med., 47*:979–989, 1957.

Kraft, I. A., Marcus, I. M., Wilson, W., Swander, D. V., Rumage, N. S., and Schulhofer, E.: Methodological problems in studying the effect of tranquilizers in children with specific reference to meprobamate. *Southern Med. J., 52*:179–185, 1959.

Krugman, A. D., Ross, S., Vicino, F. L., and Clyde, D. J.: A research note: Effects of dextroamphetamine and meprobamate on problem-solving and mood of aged subjects. *J. Geront., 15*:419–420, 1960.

Laird, D. M., Angelo, J. N., and Hope, J. M.: Evaluation of meprobamate (Miltown) in treatment of hospitalized schizophrenic patients. *Dis. Nerv. Sys., 18*:346–351, 1957.

Laties, V. G.: Effects of Meprobamate on fear and palm sweating. *J. Abnorm. Soc. Psychol., 59*: 156–161, 1959.

Lauener, H.: Conditioned suppression in rats and the effect of pharmacological agents thereon. *Psychopharmacologia, 4*:311–325, 1963.

Linzenich, H.: Meprobamate in adjustment problems of children. *Med. Klin., 53*:840–841, 1958.

Litchfield, H. R.: Clinical evaluation of meprobamate in disturbed and prepsychotic children. *Ann. N. Y. Acad. Sci., 67*:828–832, 1957.

Lorr, M., McNair, D. M., Weinstein, G. J., Michaux, W. W., and Raskin, A.: Meprobamate and chlorpromazine in psychotherapy. *Arch. Gen. Psychiat., 4*:381–389, 1961.

Lynch, V. D., Aceto, M. D., and Thoms, R. K.: The effects of certain psychopharmacologic drugs on conditioning in the rat. I. *J. Amer. Pharm. Assoc., 49*:205–210, 1960.

Mantegazzini, P., Fabbri, S., and Magni, C.: Effect of some tranquilizers on intraspecific aggressiveness in the mouse. *Arch. Ital. Sci. Farmacol., 10*:347–351, 1960.

Margolis, H. J.: Associative interference: Effects of meprobamate on normal adult's performance on a Müller-Schümann type learning task. *Psychopharmacologia, 8*:379–388, 1966.

Marriott, A. S., and Spencer, P. S. J.: Effects of centrally acting drugs on exploratory behaviour in rats. *Brit. J. Pharmacol., 25*:432–441, 1965.

Martens, S.: Clinical trial of emylcamate. A new internuncial blocking tranquilizer. A double-blind study in alcoholic outpatients. *Quart. J. Alcohol., 21*:223–232, 1960.

Masserman, J. H.: Drugs, brain and behavior: an experimental approach to experiential psychoses. *J. Neuropsychiat., 3*:S104–S113, 1962.

McDonald, R. L., and Gynther, M. D.: Effects of verbal stimuli on autonomic responsivity of medicated and non-medicated schizophrenics and character disorders. *J. Gen. Psychol., 66*:287–299, 1962.

McNair, D. M., Goldstein, A. P., Lorr, M., Cibelli, L. A., and Roth, I.: Some effects of chlordiazepoxide and meprobamate with psychiatric outpatients. *Psychopharmacologia, 7*:256–265, 1965.

Mitchell, W. A., Fox, W., and Funke, H.: Anxiety in electroshock therapy: the role of meprobamate. *J. Clin. Exper. Psychopathol., 21*:114–128, 1960.

Muhlfelder, W. J., Garcia, G. L., and Eaton, H. C.: Meprobamate as an aid in psychotherapy. *Dis. Nerv. Syst., 20*:587–590, 1959.

Niki, H.: Differential effects of two kinds of tranquilizers upon avoidance learning and fear-motivated discrimination learning. *Jap. Psychol. Res., 1*:1–13, 1960.

Olds, J., and Travis, R. P.: Effects of chlorpromazine, meprobamate, pentobarbital and morphine on self-stimulation. *J. Pharmacol. Exp. Therap., 128*:397–404, 1960.

Parigi, S., and Biagiotti, F.: Mental tests (Rorschach, Thematic Apperception Test (T. A. T.), Toulouse-Pieron) and meprobamate administration. *Riv. Pat., Nerv., 78*:1100–1103, 1957.

Park, L. C., Uhlenhuth, E. H., Lipman, R. S., Rickels, K., and Fisher, S.: A comparison of doctor and patient improvement ratings in a drug (meprobamate) trial. *Brit. J. Psychiat., 111*:535–540, 1965.

Pennington, V. M.: Use of Miltown (meprobamate) with psychotic patients. *Amer. J. Psychiat., 114*:257–260, 1957.

Perlstein, M. A.: Use of meprobamate (Miltown) in convulsion and related disorders. *J.A.M.A., 161*:1040–1044, 1956.

Plotnikoff, N.: A neuropharmacological study of escape from audiogenic seizures. *Colloq. Int. Cent. Nat. Res. Sci., 112*:429–446, 1963.

Pollard, J. C.: Combined effects of chlorpromazine and meprobamate in chronically disturbed psychotic patients. *Dis. Nerv. Syst., 20*:427–429, 1959.

Powell, B. J., Martin, L. K., and Kamano, D. K.: Effects of amobarbital sodium and meprobamate on acquisition of conditioned avoidance. *Psychol. Rep., 17*:691–694, 1965.

Rawitt, K. C.: The usefulness and effectiveness of Equanil in children. *Amer. J. Psychiat., 115*:1120–1121, 1959.

Ray, O. S.: Tranquilizer effects on conditioned suppression. *Psychopharmacologia, 4*:326–342, 1963. motivated behavior in rats.

Ray, O. S.: Tranquilizer effects on conditioned suppression. *Psychopharmacologia, 5*:136–146, 1964.

Ray, O. S.: Tranquilizer effects as a function of experimental anxiety procedures. *Arch. Int. Pharmacodyn., 153*:49–68, 1965.

Rickels, K., and Bass, H.: A comparative controlled clinical trial of seven hypnotic agents in medical and psychiatric in-patients. *Amer. J. Med. Sci., 245*:142–152, 1963.

Rickels, K., Cattell, R., MacAfee, A., and Hesbacker, P.: Drug response and important external events in the patient's life. *Dis. Nerv. Syst.*, *26*:782–786, 1965.

Rickels, K., Cattell, R. B., Weise, C., Gray, B., Yee, R., Mallin, A., and Aaronson, H. G.: Controlled psychopharmacological research in private psychiatric practice. *Psychopharmacologia, 9*:288–306, 1966.

Rickels, K., Clark, T. W., Ewing, J. H., Klingensmith, W. C., and Morris, H. M.: Evaluation of tranquilizing drugs in medical outpatients. *J. Amer. Med. Assoc., 171*:1649–1656, 1959.

Rickels, K., and Snow, L.: Meprobamate and phenobarbital sodium in anxious neurotic psychiatric and medical clinic outpatients. *Psychopharmacologia, 5*:339–348, 1964.

Rudy, L. H., Himwich, H. E., and Rinaldi, F.: A clinical evaluation of psychopharmacological agents in the management of disturbed mentally defective patients. *Amer. J. Ment. Defit., 62*:855–860, 1958.

Scriabine, A., and Blake, M.: Evaluation of centrally acting drugs in mice with fighting behaviour induced by isolation. *Psychopharmacologia, 3*:224–226, 1962.

Settel, E.: Phenaglycodol for geriatric agitation. *Geriat., 12*:607–611, 1957.

Smith, J. A., Rutherford, A., and Fanning, R.: A comparison of phenaglycodol (Ultran), meprobamate and a placebo in abstinent alcoholics. *Amer. J. Psychiat., 114*:364–365, 1957.

Solomon, P., Marcotty, A., Wexler, D., Mendelson, J., and Kubzansky, P.: Psychiatric clinical drug testing in a general hospital. *Clin. Therap. Rep.,* 691–693, 1958.

Tamura, M.: The effects of some central nervous system depressants on conflict behavior in dogs. *Jap. J. Pharmacol., 13*:133–142, 1963.

Tanabe, K.: Pharmacological studies on the conditioned response. *Yonago Acta. Med., 6*:180–184, 1963.

Tedeschi, R. E., Tedeschi, D. H., Mucha, A., Cook, L., Mattis, P. A., and Fellows, E. J.: Effects of various centrally acting drugs on fighting behavior of mice. *J. Pharmac. Exp. Therap., 125*:28–34, 1959.

Toms, E. C.: A comparative study of selected tranquilizers in the treatment of psychiatric patients. *J. Nerv. Ment. Dis., 132*:425–431, 1961.

Tucker, K., and Wilensky, H.: A clinical evaluation of meprobamate therapy in a chronic schizophrenic population. *Amer. J. Psychiat., 113*:698–703, 1957.

102

Uhlenhuth, E. H., Canter, A., Neustadt, J. O., and Payson, H. E.: The symptomatic relief of anxiety with meprobamate, phenobarbital and placebo. *Amer. J. Psychiat., 115*:905–910, 1959.

Uhlenhuth, E. H., Park, L. C., Lipman, R. S., Rickels, K., Fisher S., and Mock, J.: Dosage deviation and drug effects in drug trials. *J. Nerv. Ment. Dis., 141*:95–99, 1965.

Uhlenhuth, E. H., Rickels, K., Fisher, S., Park, L. C., Lipman, R. S., and Mock, J.: Drug, doctor's verbal attitude and clinic setting in the symptomatic response to pharmacotherapy. *Psychopharmacologia, 9*:392–418, 1966.

Uhr, L., and Miller, J. G.: Experimentally determined effects of emylcamate (Striatran) on performance, autonomic response, and subjective reactions under stress. *Amer. J. Med. Sci., 240*:204–212, 1960.

Uhr, L., and Platz, A., Fox, S. S., and Miller, J. G.: Effects of meprobamate on continuous attention behavior. *J. Gen. Psychol., 70*:51–57, 1964.

Uhr, L., Pollard, J. C., and Miller, J. G.: Behavioral effects of chronic administration of psychoactive drugs to anxious patients. *Psychopharmacologia, 1*:150–168, 1959.

Weaver, J. E., and Miya, T. S.: Effects of certain ataraxic agents on mice activity. *J. Pharm. Sci., 50*:910–912, 1961.

Werboff, J., and Havlena, J.: Postnatal behavioral effects of tranquilizers administered to the gravid rat. *Exper. Neurol., 6*:263–269, 1962.

Werboff, J., and Kesner, R.: Learning deficits of offspring after administration of tranquilizing drugs to the mothers. *Nature, 197*:106, 1963.

Zucker, A. H., Machlin, S. D., and Scott, W.: An evaluation of meprobamate in opiate withdrawal. *Amer. J. Psychiat., 115*:254–255, 1958.

Zukin, P., Arnold, D. G., and Kessler, C. R.: Comparative effects of phenaglycodol and meprobamate on anxiety reactions. *J. Nerv. Ment. Dis., 129*:193–195, 1959.

Name Index

103

Subject Index